Gringos In Paradise

DISCLAIMER

This book is not a travel guide, it is a travel adventure. And just as the person who started to write this book is not the same person that finished it, I hope your reading this true story offers you a similar experience.

For those of you that speak Spanish, I offer my apologies for my blunders as I attempted to learn. For those of you who do not speak Spanish, please do not consider this book to be a correct course of study.

Visit www.booksurge.com to order additional copies.

Gringos In Paradise
Our Honduras Odyssey

Malana Ashlie

2008

Gringos In Paradise

CONTENTS

Thank You

To our children:
James and Veronica; Mike and Monica; Rick;
Mattie and Mike; Pepper and Scott.
Your love gives us permission to spread our wings.

To our "'Ohana" for understanding our need to grow.

To don Ricardo Banegas Vasquez and la Senorita Carolina Guevara Albarenga of El Porvenir, without who's help this story could not have taken place.

To the people of Honduras, especially those of El Porvenir and La Ceiba, for their patience and support as I transitioned from the most naïve to the more accustomed.

One Reader's Impression

There's so much to enjoy about "Gringos in Paradise!"

It describes with verve the trials and tribulations of an American couple who decide to relocate from Hawai'i to Honduras with their cat. Why Honduras, of which they know close to nothing at all? They don't even speak a word of Spanish! As the author Malana Ashlie says, "call it synchronicity or divine order"....

In a lively, funny way, she invites us to peek into their multifaceted adventure....

This is a tale of courage, of respectful discovery as they draw upon their humanity and capacity to resonate with their environment to merge with a world so alien to theirs that they need to find an interpreter to go to the hardware store.... Life as an adventure in consciousness, written with feelings and with plenty of heart; Malana Ashlie is not afraid to laugh at herself, meanwhile telling us about her joys as well as her worries, fears and self-doubts. Unlike so many "gringos," she strives for a sense of peace, of harmony that can only be found through reaching inward to little-known parts of oneself, risking one's soul, previous knowledge and comfort zones. We partake in her wonderment, as she endeavors to tread lightly, to walk in balance with nature and people.

Peace is fragile and yet holds so much power....

There's so much to enjoy about "Gringos in Paradise!"

Viviane Lerner, Ph. D.
Former editor and translator,
French poet and world traveler,
Retired healer and astrologer

Introduction

We had decided to move to Honduras. Why we chose that portion or even any portion of Central America has no firm answer. My husband Ordin and I packed up our beloved cat Pueo and the barest needs to chase our dream of a peaceful and affordable lifestyle. Would this move be the answer to that dream or the source of our worst nightmare? Truth be told, little had we realized the extent to which leaving the country of our birth and culture would challenge so many of our beliefs.

International travel was not our strongest suit. Yet our five years in Hawai'i and our earlier business in Florida had given us a fair amount of experience in interacting with people of other nationalities and backgrounds. Reports from others who had relocated outside the U.S. painted pictures of a lifestyle which strengthened our research. Divine order seemed manifested when, surfing the Internet, we came across the mention of a spacious house in a little beach town called El Porvenir, along the north coast of Honduras. The ten-year-old *casa* was a block from the Caribbean Sea with a river and dock outside the rear gate. The property sat nestled in a 'Honduran beach community' only a half hour drive from an airport. Its appeal was enhanced by the address: "The two story yellow house on the beach road, past Tilapias restaurant." It sounded idyllic and the sale was closed with just the lightest inspection.

Only after our arrival in the country did we realize that even the English language can be vague. I learned the term "Honduran Community" meant no one spoke English, there was little chance of phone service, and computer connection was often faulty at best. I began to feel transported into a parallel universe, locked into the 1950s.

This was the basis for this book. It was a way to share our astounding adventure with the many people who cared for us and were convinced that we had totally lost our minds in choosing to move to Honduras. After all, we were not vibrant, young, backpacking college sorts, naively ready to challenge the world. Our families were quick to remind us that we were moderately healthy, ready-to-retire quinquagenarians that had learned to appreciate a cushy lifestyle. Writing became a way to process my thoughts and emotions as I waded into these uncharted waters.

The famous American author Mark Twain once stated: "Travel is fatal to prejudice, bigotry, and narrow-mindedness, and many of our people need it sorely on these accounts. Broad, wholesome, charitable views of men and things cannot be acquired by vegetating in one little corner of the earth all one's lifetime."

On the days when I could not see my blessings I clung to those words. Like many others, I took pride in being open-minded and accepting of others. However, the rules, regulations and lawsuits that were a staple of my previous culture left little room to test this self-concept. How would I respond if my perceptions became challenged? Could I release my programmed need for security to live life with the freedom of reliance my forefathers taught? After all, safe is not necessarily free.

What about the language problem? It had been my longtime desire to speak Spanish, but I had lacked the motivation to make the dream a reality; now it would be a necessity. Was it possible for my brain, complacent in its need for only one language, to integrate a new tongue?

The decision to relocate would also test my belief that dealing with people from the heart could transcend language barriers. Our wish was not to live as outsiders in a foreign land, limiting our contacts to others of our kind while clinging to the comforts of a past life. Ordin and I realized that this would require that we put aside many of our stateside views and accept a more Honduran attitude: after all, wasn't this part of why we were here?

The allure of opportunity once beckoned pirates and conquistadors to these shores and the same sea breezes that brought them here now sang the ballads of adventure to my soul.

If we held fast to our dream and navigated the rough, could we make the transition?

After all, how difficult could it be?

Ah, sweet home, Honduras....

Malana Ashlie

SECTION I

The Decision

The Gringos

The Hawaiian morning was postcard-perfect as my husband Ordin and I said our last good-bye to friends and loaded our scant amount of luggage into the van. Combing my fingers through my short brown hair, I folded my long frame into the copilot's seat and turned to receive the blue mesh cat carrier from Ordin's hands. I wondered how we would look back on this decision. We were moving to Honduras. Of all the crazy things that we had done in our fourteen years of marriage, this was either the craziest or the most brilliant. Only time would tell.

Waving good-bye as we backed out of the driveway, I found my mind exploring how we had come to this point in time. I looked at Ordin seated next to me, lips set in a thin line of determination with hands planted firmly on the steering wheel; residual habits from his years as a police officer. Yet these images of inflexibility were belied by the curly gray ponytail and slippered feet he had adopted during our years on the island. An inventive scholar by nature but not necessarily a long-range planner, his genius came from being singularly focused. Ordin has always been a pretty grounded guy, living out his first twenty some years around the area of his birth in Pennsylvania, and another thirty plus on the Gulf Coast of Florida. His approach to life is fairly cerebral with the trained mind of a critical thinker. It must have been his short tour of military duty in Hawai'i that awakened his desire to seek paradise.

In contrast, I'm more of a feeler, plus I'd rather see the glass half-full than try to figure out where the leak is. It's incredible that I'm as grounded as I am since wanderlust seems to be in my blood. The Grapes of Wrath novel cannot conjure more graphic images than my memories of a stringy-haired, brown-eyed girl squeezed between three to five brothers in the backseat of a "48" Desoto. The touch of the worn gray flannel upholstery is as real as the memories of tussling for window positions that would offer the first view of the new place and the next school. I saw my parents nomadic wandering as a harsh jolt to my tender self-image, and I was sure that every hardship of my young life was because of my father's itchy feet.

The more resilient part of my personality recognized that each new location represented a new beginning; an opportunity to erase a portion of my history. However, the results of being planted in and plucked from various schools also left me with a sense of loneliness; a vague feeling of being outside. All of this erasing had also whisked away much of my self-identity. It is the nature of most parents to want for their children what they felt their own childhood lacked, so once my children were born I was on a crusade to find a place for them to put down roots.

It soon became obvious the best intentions cannot override DNA. Migrant tendencies were my nature so that no matter how I applied logic, the inclination would delude my thinking. By the time the youngest of my three was in first grade, their father and I were contemplating our sixth move and this time I was convinced the Tri-Lakes area of the Ozark Mountains would be the best place. The mountains, rivers, forest and people awakened a deep sense of belonging within me on my first trip there. Nonetheless, as close to perfection as the area seemed, fate had other plans. Within six years, the marriage which was challenged before the move, had ended. Another five years later found me living on the Gulf Coast of Florida, reexamining my life.

It was there that I met Ordin. We were part of a circle of single friends that had evolved over a period of months. Many of us were striving to create a sense of balance after the disastrous results of divorce and resulting bankruptcy. Neither Ordin nor I were seeking new life partners and looking back on our first meeting, I still remember my wonder at his reluctance to muster forth any effort toward warmth or charm. Poor thing, I was sure that if he ever wanted to find a partner he would find himself low on anyone's eligibility list.

At this point in our lives our respective children were on their own, which offered freedom to examine our beliefs and explore what we wanted from life. This was an opportunity to look outside the sheltered thinking of my youth and explore the traditions and beliefs of other cultures. Ordin and I found that we had this interest in common and gradually, out of our circle of friends, we became best friends. We took classes and looked into new thought together. At first it was more my suggestion triggering his interest, and then it became his pursuit as much as mine. Not long afterwards, we decided to compose marriage vows that would contain the promise to keep exploring; we swore to keep our life together a voyage of adventure.

Our first shared venture was the study of Naturopathic healing. I had studied with a native herbalist in the Ozarks years before I ever met Ordin and so it was easy to support his efforts in completing a degree as a Doctor of Naturopathy. He had been working in construction since leaving law enforcement; it had fed his stomach but not his soul. My ten-year career as a Sales Director with a large cosmetic company was a profitable choice for my gregarious tendencies but my life experiences were teaching me that some problems required more than cover-up. Natural Health was an opportunity to serve at a different level.

The St. Petersburg/Clearwater area of Florida was a fertile ground for holistic therapies and our studies went well. We opened a clinic within walking distance of our home and I resigned my sales commission. For several years Ordin and I stayed busy teaching, seeing clients and expanding our knowledge. The area grew and business thrived. Yet, the sun, sand and ocean were no longer sufficient trade-offs for the traffic, noise and crowds. When I found myself critically focused on the changes, a silent place within me would often whisper, "It's only temporary." While Florida did not feel like home, it did not seem the time to move on. There was still something that held me there.

As one of the gateways to the U.S., Florida is home for various nationalities and the belief systems by which they live. This assembly creates a multicultural soup, so to speak, and the various customs and religions practiced continued to intrigue me. Studying the philosophies of cultures from around the globe offered opportunities to weigh my own values. This exposure was also the basis for the decision to gift myself with an astrology reading for my fiftieth birthday.

The astrologers name was Stella; I had seen her flyer posted on the door of the New Age shop where Ordin and I bought essential oils. She leased a small space for her readings in an adjoining room and happened to have an opening on the day I visited the store. There was an hour to wait so I gave my birth information to the storeowner. It was entered into a computer and within moments a natal chart was placed into my hands. It showed the placement of stars and planets at the time of my birth. My instructions were to give it to the astrologer when my appointment began. My mind filled with chatter as I strolled along the aisles of cards, candles, and other goods while awaiting my appointed hour. The thrill of curiosity, supported by my changing belief system was challenging the inner voices of my old religious training. The clash created a slight sensation of butterflies fluttering in my stomach. As the appointment time arrived the door opened. I am not sure if I had expected to see someone draped in bangles and beads but the figure before me was an attractive young woman dressed conservatively in comfortable, summer apparel. Her appearance was so conventional that I might not have given her a second thought if I passed her in the grocery store. She offered her hand saying, "I'm Stella, are you Malana?" Immediately my butterflies settled into formation. Her voice was clear and reassuring with an air of professionalism, her gentle manner put me at ease. She made small talk as she guided me into her reading room, eventually asking if I were in search of any specific information.

With the preliminaries over we sat at a small table and Stella started a timer. She began by studying the chart I had given her and within just a few moments started pointing out stars and planets that opposed or supported my character traits. I was vaguely aware of some of this information from my own studies while other parts of it made no sense to me at all. Just as I was beginning to wonder if the time would be worth the money I had paid Stella stated, "I believe you have always felt an outsider in your own family." I was stunned with the realization, "She knows my secret!" Her next words confirmed this as she added, "You have always longed for a sense of home." Her spoken words cast light into the hidden recesses of wounds I had learned to ignore. Tears filled my eyes. She continued to study the chart further and then offered, "You are a child of the universe, Malana; the entire planet is meant to be your home." I felt a weight suddenly lifted from my shoulders and replaced by a sense of peace. For years I had been trying to fit in, be accepted, when in reality uniqueness was my norm. There was nothing wrong with ME, I was OK the way I was. This new insight gave me permission to fly.

That day felt as though the earth had stopped spinning on its axis and abruptly changed direction. After all the years of trying to find a home, I finally understood that home is always with me. This was what all the study, exploration and searching had been leading me to discover. After ten years on the Florida Coast it was now time to spread my wings and move on; I just needed a direction. Ordin and I discussed our options and decided to head for Hawai'i. We had been taking groups to the islands on health retreats for the last couple of years. Those trips had rekindled his dream of returning to live in Hawai'i. His short tour of duty there had answered a call that Pennsylvanian conventionality had muffled. However, as we began to research the move we found it might be more difficult than we thought. The saying "You can never go back." proved to be true. We searched for beaches he had visited, people he had known, and prices that had once existed; all of which seemed to have vaporized and been carried off by the winds of change. For a while we considered Maui as a possible alternative, but in the time it took us to make the decision and get our affairs in order, the island became priced out of our market. We were not baby boomers who had struck it rich on the stock market; we were in the boomer group with credit card debt and little savings. These conditions seemed intensified when we learned that new health laws adopted by Hawai'i would restrict us from using our naturopathic degrees; another discouraging setback. Neither of us wanted to give up the plan but it was difficult to discern if these obstacles were barriers or signals to alter our path. After talking, my meditating and his surfing the Internet, we decided to hang onto the dream but explore another island.

Since all aspects of holistic healing were gaining popularity, we believed that if we could just plant our feet on a black sand beach we would find our niche. That belief brought us to choose the Big Island of Hawai'i. We liked the Hilo area because of its laid-back family atmosphere and easy affordability. Moving from the bustle of a metropolis we were in search of a quieter place with a feeling of community. As we explored along the eastern coastline, we found friendly people, beautiful flora, and values that were close to our hearts. It seemed perfect. This green side of the Big Island offered our nerves a soothing balm with its lush vegetation and breathtaking waterfalls. The lower, non-tourist economy of that area fit right into our pocketbook, and the warm aloha spirit of the locals made us feel welcomed as 'Ohana; family of the heart. We downsized our possessions, found a freight company and said good-bye to Florida.

Island life was soon as comfortable to us as the open rubber slippers that most local folks wore. We bought a house and settled into the community. We even increased the size of our family with the addition of a one and a half pound tortoiseshell calico feline which we named Pueo. We thought that life could not be more perfect, but soon found that perfection was elusive and nothing stands still. Within five years our paradise began to change. Weather changes everywhere around the world were also cooling our area of the island. The more frequent rains, with cooler nights, were making our 30-year, single-wall, plantation-style home cooler than we found comfortable. Compounding that condition, baby boomers seeking a change while the interest rates were low were turning our area of paradise into tropical suburbia. Our rubber "slippah" comfort had taken on the pinch of new leather shoes. The empty acres of jungle that had insulated us no longer existed. Contractors followed bulldozers and we found ourselves surrounded by barren acres with mainland style houses popping up on either side. The upside of all of this was that our little plantation-style house had tripled in value and its sale gave us the freedom to look at our options.

If we were to leave, where would we go? Hawai'i makes an impression within you that can never be erased. We would want to find a place where the pace was slow, the weather warm, the beaches uncluttered, and it would need to be priced affordably. The recent mortgage boom had knocked most of the coastal area of the U.S. out of our picture. Ordin and I decided to spin the office globe to see what was available. We were looking for paradise but had already learned that paradise was tenuous; like reaching for a star. However, we had also learned that the thrill of life comes from trying to grasp what may seem unattainable. If we don't keep reaching we have failed to live.

Where in the World...?

Not all the changes we felt were restricted to our environment. The families we had left on the mainland were going through transitions as well. My parents' health had begun a rapid decline; new grandchildren had expanded established families and the fathers were scheduled for Iraq. It seemed sensible to reduce the distance that created a 17-hour air flight but the problem was in choosing the right location. A return to Florida's white sand coastline was the first thought; Ordin's children were still there, but so was the noise and congestion. Friends warned us that new construction had created condominium complexes that blocked out the shoreline, plus the increase of recent hurricane traffic to that coast made it less than inviting.

My family in the Ozarks had now spread throughout the Midwest and my parents were no longer in their home. My children, well established, had the same sense of independence that my parents had instilled in me; they were self-reliant and seldom asked for help. My emotions felt shredded as I wavered between wanting to be available for family and yet not wanting to enable parents or children by interfering. Do I need to be there? If not, then how far away is too far? What about the promise that O and I had made to each other? Was there a compromise? Was it possible to please both sides? My sense of peace became shattered by the constant internal interrogation. For three months I wrestled with these questions, seeking answers that would bring me peace.

Over the years, since my holistic and subtle energy studies began, a certain level of intuition and understanding has developed that I use successfully to help others, but it was totally inaccessible to me through this cloud of emotional turmoil. Ordin, on the other hand, though somewhat intuitive, works as a problematic thinker. Most of his suggestions seemed callous, coming from his logical perspective, so I stopped seeking his advice. Overwhelmed with emotions, my meditations became muddled, my prayers perplexed. Finally, out of the state of confusion, I remembered a practice that I commonly teach to clients. This process allows one to step outside emotional havoc and become the observer. Once I had achieved this place of calm, I began to see that my greatest responsibility was simply to make myself available. Family would ask for help if they wanted it; for me to step in without being asked could be construed as interfering.

This luminescence brought me such a wonderful sense of peace and direction that I immediately went to share it with O. I was sure that my partner's concern for my emotional well-being had him in almost as great apprehension as I was. I wanted to share my epiphany as well as soothe his concern and ease his worry. I found him in his office sitting at the computer, oblivious to my weeks of distress. He had been merrily surfing the internet for information on Costa Rica.

It seems that life in Costa had been the topic of conversation at the weekly Hilo market for a while and stirred his curiosity. What he had heard intrigued him and he wanted to research the country for himself. Costa Rica's political stability had impressed him, along with his findings on the economic and judicial systems. Costa was becoming an interesting possibility. Neither of us had ever considered living outside the U.S. but we knew many Americans were doing just that. The distance by air to where our family members live was less than half of that from Hawai'i, plus real estate in the country seemed affordable. As the research continued we found that finding an area that would match our wishes to the conditions available could be a challenge. The Pacific side would mean higher prices and cooler water temperatures, while the Atlantic side offered warmer water but not our style of living. Then, just as in the past, we took long enough to wrestle over the decision that conditions there began to change. Prices started to rise due to the increasing number of Americans and Europeans that were flooding into the Pacific coast area of Costa Rica.

As frustrating as that was, we found that once we had broken through the limiting idea of living only within the U.S. borders, a new doorway opened and we were again ready to consider our choices. We dusted off the office globe and scanned the multicolored shapes to renew our knowledge of Central American geography. Since our interest had become centered on the Caribbean side with easy access to the U.S., our search narrowed. We hovered over the globe, our fingers tracing the contours of Mexico and its neighbors to the south. Belize peaked my interest first as it had held an appeal for me during my high school years. Anywhere along the white sand beaches of the Yucatan would get my vote since it would simplify the studies I had begun among Maya elders just a couple of years before. As our fingers continued to trace, they finally came to meet on Honduras.

Ordin and I looked at each other with the same question in our minds: what did we know about this country? Neither he nor I had heard much for many years...not since the coups of the seventies. Then a flash of memory brought back the face of a young woman we had met just a couple of years before we left Florida; she was Honduran. I remember my feelings of admiration as I studied the classic features of her face the day we met. Her facial appearance reminded me of a picture of an Egyptian queen I had seen painted on papyrus. As we got to know her better we came to realize that her attractiveness was not limited to her physical appearance; her beauty was also within. She was a woman sensitive to others suffering and was always willing to do what she could to help. In conversations, she would share stories of her youth and what her life had been like growing up around San Pedro Sula. These stories offered insight to the conditions that existed in her native country during her childhood, as well as giving insight to the character of the people. During the season that she shared our lives, seeds were innocently planted. O and I had not heard anything from or about her since that time, but we were beginning to believe the seeds she planted had begun to sprout.

I left my explorer to his investigations. O loves a mystery and happily becomes absorbed in research for hours. His querying mind will delve through layers of information until placing the last puzzle piece and the last obscurity revealed. He was the perfect Lewis or Clark to launch this fact-finding mission. By the end of the day he reported that, similar to our young woman friend, Honduras had been slowly healing from its past. The internal strife of years gone by resolved with the decision to become a democracy. Its friendly people, uncrowded beaches, history and culture, as well as the exchange rate, were beckoning to tourists. The new government had a keen interest in sharing its culture while preserving history through eco-tourism. This all made a positive impression on Ordin and me. Living around tourist areas for many years, we had burned-out long ago on congested amusement parks and major tourist attractions.

Honduras, like an adolescent awakening to its full potential, was opening its arms to the world. The beauty and mystery that drew Spanish explorers and pirates to its shores extended toward the world to experience. The more of his research he shared with me, the more it seemed like we were learning about a place lost in time. It was affordable, and its north shore on the Caribbean was only two-and-a-half hours from Houston or Miami. Two things were imminent: 1) we needed to go see it for ourselves, and 2) it was time to get a bilingual dictionary. Honduras was beckoning.

The Sleuths

Call it synchronicity or divine order; I am always in awe as I watch the universe create forces that make sense out of what appears as chaos. Even during times that I have not consciously chosen a direction, some cosmic force seems to be laying the stepping-stones that support my yet-to-be- realized wishes. Two-and-a-half years before our move to Honduras, I was offered an opportunity to travel into Guatemala to study the Mayan Calendar as a student of traditional Elders. Maya history had been an interest of mine since high school so I jumped at the opportunity. Seven months later, I was attending a metaphysical convention in Sedona where I met a charismatic man named Oscar Reconco. He lived outside Las Vegas in the desert town of Pahrump but traveled around the world connecting with dolphin energy for healing. Although a U.S. citizen, he was Honduran by birth. He had come to America after graduating from college to work as the administrator of a medical clinic. After having a unique experience with dolphins in the wild, he left the field of medical science for one of metaphysics. A mutual respect and a similar interest in spiritual retreats gave us common ground for friendship and we immediately clicked. Later, as Ordin and I began considering Honduras as a possible home, I made a point to reconnect with Oscar to probe him for information. Pleased that I had called him, he told me that he was less than a month away from a trip to Kona on the west side of our island, and he would arrange time to visit us and answer all our questions. Having him stay at the house would also give him some insight to our lifestyle and if it could adapt to Honduras living.

The late afternoon sun was setting behind the sleeping Mauna Kea volcano when Oscar pulled into the drive. It was good to see him again. His Kona business was finished and he would be able to kick back and enjoy his short time with us. Ordin, Oscar, my Hawaiian friend Flo and I were sitting around a table on the lanai, "local style", sharing conversation and food. We asked questions about Honduras to fill in the missing pieces left from what we had gathered. Oscar's love for his country was obvious as he would speak of the culture or describe the beauty of the mountains and countryside. Much of what he told us seemed so akin to the things we loved about Hawai'i that I was just about ready to pack. His expertise as a storyteller had us hanging on his words, waiting to hear the outcome of some unique experience. Our reactions would invariably delight him enough to bring a burst of laugher that would resound throughout the jungle clearing. As the evening became late, his narrative took on a more serious note. He cautioned me that no matter how much he loved his home, it was not for everyone. The only way to know was to visit the country ourselves. He suggested the three of us travel into Honduras together; he would act as our guide and let us get a sense of what life would be like there. I was dumbfounded. What an amazingly generous offer. To me, it was insightful of this man's personality and confirmed what we were learning of the qualities of Hondurans. Much of what we had read showed the majority were sociable and willing to help. Of course, even Oscar admitted that many his countrymen also had a Robin Hood complex, in that they might rob from the rich to give (or sell) to the poor, but if you asked for help, they would assist.

Ordin and I agreed that a personal inspection of the country was vital and I did not feel that we should pass up Oscars offer to escort, but there was one slight obstacle to both of us going. It was a small, furry obstacle. For four years our lives have been controlled and rewarded by a soft ball of fur that we have spoiled beyond tolerance, at least beyond anyone else's ability to tolerate. The name of the feline who rules our lives is Pueo, which is the Hawaiian word for owl. She is a dark, tortoiseshell calico with caramel markings and she was the only one of her coloring in the basket of rowdy little kittens being given away at the Hilo market one day. As I lifted the towel covering the plastic laundry basket that held them, Pu looked up at me from the semi-darkness, her big ears and the golden-brown circles around her eyes giving her all the look of her namesake. At that moment she was pinned down by three of the others. As much as she may have appeared in need of protection from her sibs, she was not sure the giants peering over the edge of her basket were a better alternative. Now she is ten pounds of regal felinity. Her nature is somewhat timid and she has learned to rely on her dark coloring as perfect camouflage for deep shadows, nightfall and early morning. In our desire to protect her, Ordin claims that we have pampered her beyond simply spoiled rotten; she has become "compost." Anyone whose life is ruled by a pet will know exactly what I am describing. Still, we love her and are willing to live with her demands. The only real problem with indulging her is that we have taken her far beyond finding any assistance in her care: she prefers her tuna hand-fed.

When Ordin and I moved to Hawai'i, it was just the two of us. Our only emotional support came from each other. That move was a step in faith since we had no contacts on the island or any direction to turn for help. Conversely, the islands are not really a foreign country and we could, almost, understand the local language. Considering a move that required a passport was a much larger step, so to have a friend at our side would be a definite advantage; especially a friend who knew his way around. Since only one of us would be making the trip into Honduras with Oscar, we decided that it should be Ordin. The dynamic duo, OO, would DO Honduras together; we girls would hold the fort.

Oscar's offer to leave his business to make the ten-day journey through Honduras was no simple task. He had a retail store, a church, and a weekly television program, as well as doing counseling. His offer required him to leave his retail store in the hands of trusted friends, prerecord his television program and find someone to replace him in leading his church service. He is a dynamic personality and how he manages all he does is a mystery to anyone who watches him in action. His move to the U.S. came after graduating from college. He went to explore the opportunities available with a desire to assist his family. It was only after he moved to the Las Vegas area that he began the spiritual healing ministry that he has today. This is what he was offering to leave in meeting Ordin at the Las Vegas airport. From there, their itinerary would take them to Tegucigalpa, the capital of Honduras, where they would meet with Oscar's family and friends and make the introductions that could offer direction.

The Great Exploration

The international phone call from Ordin reported the flight, although long, had gone well. After a couple of days of visiting lawyers and checking regulations in the capital city, the guys met with Oscar's college mate, José. He would be their driver through the mountains to the north shore of the country—the Caribbean coast. With all of our investigation, and my intuition, we had focused on the area of La Ceiba, give or take twenty miles on either side. This meant they had the coast to explore in the area between Tela and the old capital of Trujillo. La Ceiba, situated in the middle, is a newer city neatly planned around a town square and the home of Spring Festival, the biggest celebration of its kind this side of Rio de Janeiro. Ceiba is also a wonderful shopping metropolis, with street vendors and shops offering cool fresh fruit juices, clothing, furniture or any other item you may wish. Tela, to the west, is considered a party town because of its large expanse of beaches. When the fruit companies pulled out of that area, the effect on the community was devastating. It has never fully recovered but has wonderful potential. Trujillo, to the east, is one of the oldest towns on the Caribbean coast. It was the original capital for Honduras; its streets are narrow and it has preserved its old-world charm. The government chose to move the capital to the Pacific coast after repeated blockades by pirates.

José's expertise behind the wheel was a blessing. After twenty years of living in the U.S., Oscar refused to drive in Honduras. It is definitely not for the fainthearted. Posted speed limits are flexible, enforcement of the speed is minimal, potholes are terminal and horns are mandatory for turns, passing and at intersections. Various numbers of horses and cows graze the vegetation along the sides of the roads, crossing at a whim, while bicyclists and pedestrians navigate through the taxi and auto congestion. The occasional horseback rider or horse drawn cart are accepted modes of transport and give support to the chaos theory. School buses and taxis are everywhere. Public transportation is always available but an understanding of the language is a plus. Not all school buses are what they would seem. Rather than transporting swarms of children, they carry adults from town to town. Have you ever given any thought to what happened to the old buses from your school days? Well, you may find them traveling the roads of Honduras. The need to block out the letters and repaint them is not an issue, so buses unwittingly champion schools from Albuquerque to Mt. Zion, while serving multitudes of Hondurans in their travels to work or shop.

It was a three-hour drive through the mountains from the capital to San Pedro Sula, where the route turned east and headed for La Ceiba. José was driving Honduran style, which varies from tailgating to high-speed passing. Fuel, at over three dollars a gallon, needed to conservation, so José saved the air-conditioning only for the rainy periods when it would help keep the windows clear. The sun was warm and the traffic exhaust ever apparent as they wound their way toward the high mountains. Between the humidity and the perspiration from traveling on warm vinyl seats, Ordin's attitude was tempered only by the good humor and amusing stories swapped by the three men as they wound their way up into the mountains.

Suddenly, his discomfort gave way to wonder and amazement as his eyes took in the panorama around him. The scene was majestic mountains covered with large mahogany and deep-root pine trees that instilled an almost sacred feeling. Ordin stared through the window in awe, humbled by these ancient trees that bore witness to the passage of time. The forest continued as the highway serpentined along ridges and valleys, following the natural pattern of the terrain. The sun was still shy of its zenith as the travelers left the forest and started their descent. It was time to think about lunch as they reached a fork in the highway and took the turn to La Ceiba. Refueling themselves and the car was now the top priority before continuing the remaining three-and-a-half hours to their destination.

All needs satisfied, the miles began melting away on the final leg of the journey. The highway made a curve that signaled they were now following the coast. Oscar pointed out the window and shouted "Ocean!" over the force of wind blowing through the windows from the sixty-mile- an-hour pace. Ordin narrowed his eyes to peer through the blurring palm nut groves, hoping to catch sight of water on the other side. He had recognized as a youth that saltwater gave him a deep sense of peace. Ever since he was old enough to make his own decisions, he had made choices that always kept him connected to saltwater. Now, as a stranger in a foreign land, he needed the reassurance that it was there. When they came to the intersection at Ceiba, Ordin tapped José and directed him toward the beach. "Ahh, salt air." Ordin said as the car stopped at the beach access. "This is what we're looking for." It took only moments for him to cross the brown sand beach and wade into the turquoise water of the Caribbean. He had come home. Many of the things he had loved about Hawai'i, Florida, and even the Atlantic City of his childhood, whispered to him as he stood thigh deep in the water that afternoon. It had all seemed different and foreign until he reached the North Coast. This area had possibilities.

The water felt wonderful and the weather was fantastic. It was the perfect reward for a long, hot day of traveling. Now they would find a room for the night and be ready to scout the area in the morning. Ordin's quest, at this point, was to determine if our intuition had been right about the area and, if so, locate available housing for us to rent. We felt renting would allow us more time to explore the area before making a purchase. The day was winding to a close when the three weary travelers checked into the Grand Hotel Paris. After a meal and a couple of rounds of *cervezas*, they bought a newspaper and headed for their room.

The ocean and the beers had taken the edge off their weariness so, with classified ads and real estate phone numbers, the three men sat down to lay out a schedule for the next couple of days. All seemed to be going well until Odin reached for his wallet to retrieve a phone number. The wallet was gone! Mentally retracing their steps, he was momentarily thankful that he made it a habit to separate money, cards and ID when he was traveling. Most of his money, his passport and a photocopy of his other ID were still in his money belt. He carried his international credit card and daily spending money in his zippered pants pocket. There was only one thousand Lempiras in the wallet, but it did contain the rest of his identification and another credit card. Ordin realized he had last seen it when he paid for the gas and lunch at the station outside San Pedro Sula, four hours away. Anxiety burned away any residual of weariness as Ordin dashed down the stairs and out of the building to the car in search of the missing article. Discouraged and empty-handed, he reported to his friends that he would need to find an internet café to call Hawai'i and report the missing cards. There was no sense in trying to drive back now and not one of the men could remember the name of the gas station to try to call. A local phone call determined the police office that handled this type of situation was not open at night. That made their best course of action to get a good night's sleep and file a report in the morning.

Filling out the police report became a two-day job since the department that files this particular "international type" report is only open during certain hours of the day and exists in only one specific location within the city. As our three amigos asked for directions, it seemed there was a bit of confusion among the local police officers about exactly where that office was located. After traveling back and forth from one end of town to another, from one station to another, the men finally located the proper office within the proper police division. The sign on the door stated that this department took only certain types of complaints during certain times on specific days. A second sign announced "Closed for lunch, come back in two hours." They could not change government policy and lunch seemed like a good idea, so they went for something to eat with plans to stop at a real estate office they had passed in their morning travels. The local eateries were packed so the posted lunch time was just about over when the men headed back to the station. They wanted to be there a little early to expedite the process, but so did everyone else. Oscar did his best to find someone who could handle their special case immediately but the sour-faced person waiting at the end of the very long line mumbled that the complaints were handled on a first-come, first-serve basis.

The whole process was a physically and emotionally exhausting education; certainly not one Ordin would want to go through again. With only one day left, he had to contact real estate agents and see what he could find. The agency he had passed while pursuing police reports had the same two-hour lunch custom, so when his afternoon of standing in line was over, he had missed them completely. He had printed out a real estate agent's website page from his computer before he left Hawai'i and, with the help of his two companions, managed to find the office not far from where they were staying. The agent, Kenton Ownbey, was an American who had been living in Honduras for many years. Ordin explained our plans and our needs and asked if he could see some rental property that might be available. The response to his question added to his Honduran education: the leasing laws in the country require a three-day notice to the tenant.

A Yellow House

Ordin was exhausted by the time he returned to Hawai'i from his ten-day dash through Honduras; however, his exhaustion was intertwined with excitement and satisfaction with all he had seen. He was also feeling a bit distressed about the approaching end of our current lease. We had an agreement with the man who bought our house to allow us to rent it from him for a year while we decided what we were going to do. Now we had only a few short months left for that decision, and make the move. All of this emotional mayhem only added to his fatigue.

This is where my husband and I deal with things differently. I have a tendency to handle situations with prayer, rituals and meditation; he on the other hand, although intuitive, has an amazing intellect that he generally prefers over intuition. I'm a "let it happen" person and he is a "make it happen" type. The two styles actually complement each other well. I set up the arena and he is the catalyst that gets it all done. That does not mean there is never a time when the two methods do not grind and make sparks fly, but this was not one of them.

Since he had flown all night and had inspections lined up for the next day, I suggested that Ordin get some sleep. Meanwhile, since my mind was on the immediate problem, there was no sense in trying to do any other work. I clicked on the internet to try my luck. Ordin's approach, correctly, had been to search for "Real Estate in La Ceiba Honduras"; my style was to enter "Homes for Sale in La Ceiba". The front page of the website that appeared on the screen showed a house that almost took my breath away. It was beautiful, near the beach and affordable. All of this seemed too good to be true...but it was the house we ended buying just outside La Ceiba.

It was a "For sale by Owner" site, so we would never have found the place through a real estate agent, and it met every desire we had. It was in a beach community called El Porvenir, just twenty minutes outside La Ceiba. The house was a block-and-a-half from the Caribbean and had a spring-fed river with a dock just outside the back gate. The webpage advertisement stated that this ten-year-old house, with its wrap-around veranda and view of the mountains, was located on over a half-acre of property. I could not believe my eyes as I read down the list of amenities and came to the price. All of this, with over five thousand square feet under roof, was less than one hundred thousand dollars! That was the end of Ordin's nap; I was too excited to wait for him to awaken. I impatiently stood by the printer waiting for it to robotically complete its task, then snatched the top copy and ran down the hall to the bedroom. It took a bit of jostling to finally drag him from the realms of deep sleep, but as the impact of my words, "I've found the place, I've found the place!" penetrated his alpha state, his red-rimmed eyes began to open. The print-out from my computer was inches from his face as his heavy eyelids lifted and his vision cleared. His hand groped the bedside table in search of his glasses, while he grumbled something about being too tired to play around. "This had better be worth the loss of sleep." he mumbled. After scanning the paper, he sat up to read it again. "Wow! This definitely had possibilities." He got out of bed and headed for his office phone to make an international call to the real estate agent and developer he had met in Ceiba. In moments they were in contact and Ordin explained the situation. Kent agreed to act as our agent and guide us through the steps needed if we chose to buy the property. His first suggestion was that we contact the owner to make sure the property was still available.

The response from the owner was in my computer mailbox the next morning. The house was still for sale. The upstairs of the house was vacant, other than a small amount of furniture. The problem of our dwindling Hawai'i lease could be solved with this purchase since it would be available for us at closing. The current owner was even open to negotiating for the furniture, which would save us the expense of having to buy some immediately or staying at a hotel while we found some. The property caretaker had been living in the apartments below the house and was willing to stay on until we could move there. Kent told us he would examine the house and then e-mail his opinion. Days passed while we waited for word from five thousand miles away. Schedules and weather were causing complications, and complications meant delays. The owners of the property had moved to the U.S., allowing a young relative to live in the house, but the birth of a baby and other considerations had required her to leave El Porvenir for La Ceiba. The caretaker had been trying to contact her but she worked a schedule that seemed difficult to predict. With that delay, it was still the rainy season on the north coast and weather was restricting travel.

As we sat in the middle of the Pacific Ocean, checking for emails every day, Kent finally pulled all the ends together in Honduras and visited the property. His report was positive but with a degree of reservation. He felt the house was well worth the asking price and could bring much more if it was within the city limits of La Ceiba. The neighborhood was good, "based on Honduran standards." The house was in a Honduran neighborhood, and although he had enjoyed the years in his first home surrounded by Honduran families, Kent realized the difference in cultures can make it uncomfortable for many Americans. He was not sure what we were expecting along those lines. Honduras has no zoning, so besides the farm across the road and the beach bar a few blocks away, what potential neighbors were we willing to accept? We trusted his feedback on the house and neighborhood and felt safe enough to take the next step. He presented our offer to the owners, contingent on our making a visual inspection; once this was accepted, O was on a plane again.

The Professional

Ordin was more than qualified to inspect the house and surrounding area. He had become certified as a home inspector after we moved to Hawai'i. He made the decision to take a sabbatical from the healing arts and go back to a construction-related field when the housing boom struck Hawai'i. "Less hand-holding; more income." he said. Surprisingly, the two fields complemented each other since this new endeavor, with his experiences in the previous field, helped him set up a very effective protocol for orderly inspections. However, one of his policies was that no one should inspect his or her own house. An emotionally detached professional should always be called to offer an unbiased assessment. At this writing, home inspectors are almost nonexistent in Honduras. Kent felt that we needed to see the condition of this ten-year-old house for ourselves, so Ordin cast policy to the wind, broke his own rule and returned to Honduras to inspect his own house. We had ten days to get this done.

Another inspection rule that my husband clings to is the inspector needs solitude to examine the property. Since the assessment is a mental "troubleshooting" exercise, the inspector needs to get into his own mental space. Points of inspection take on a natural flow of thought—like movement in a dance, taking the professional from one particular point to its natural conclusion. Ordin's experience has shown that when a prospective buyer wants to be present at the inspection, it is best to schedule the meeting for the last hour. In that way, the inspector's concentration is not broken and the client can still review and view the information. That is the ideal scenario; now here is what happened.

It had only been a couple of weeks since the last trip, so Ordin was not too enthusiastic about being away from island business again. This trip was essential but his dislike of traveling and concern about business played heavily on his mind. He did not want to be away any longer than necessary. That concern, added to the excitement he was feeling about the possibility of the new home, an amount of anxiety involved in moving to a foreign country, plus the self-induced pressure of wanting to secure our future through this inspection, were all working together to create an emotional roller-coaster ride. Added to this was the pressure of trying to project his schedule to make the most of the available hours. The arena all of this was creating was not the most fertile ground in which to plant the seeds of change. He planned to fly out of Honolulu on Thursday, meet with Kent on Friday, complete the inspection and contact the lawyer, then fly back home on Saturday evening.

The first flaw in the plan came when the airline schedule required him to stay in Honduras until Sunday evening. "An entire dead day." he grumbled, but later decided the rest might do him good and he could just reschedule his Monday inspections. The second flaw centered on the inspection itself. He had already secured his tickets before he learned the present owners wanted their relative to attend the inspection and the appointment would need to fit not only her work schedule but the baby's schedule. How frustrating! He still needed time to meet with the lawyer. How much time would he need to allow for that? He had been keeping Saturday free, hoping that would do. The relative, Kenton, and Ordin all agreed that Friday afternoon at one o'clock would work, which would still leave Saturday for the legal appointment. Everything was set; all the international calls completed. It looked good to go. Ordin relaxed, feeling that everything was in order...until his eyes fell to his flight schedule on the desk. He was on a red-eye flight out of Honolulu! In his haste he had not considered this; he would not even arrive in La Ceiba until four-thirty Friday afternoon, four hours after the scheduled time for the inspection! The time difference made it impossible to contact Kent to make changes now; it would need to wait until the following day.

The e-mail that Ordin received before he left Hawai'i confirmed that Kent had been able to contact everyone and reschedule the inspection. By the end of the day, overwhelmed with weariness, Ordin stepped off the small commuter plane at La Ceiba airport. He had just enough energy left to grab something to eat before he found his room at the Grand Hotel Paris. This was the same place where he stayed with Oscar and José, and it was situated in close to Kent's office. The next morning there should be no obstacles to arriving at the office with plenty of time to go over details before they made the drive to El Porvenir.

Ordin was carrying a list of questions that he hoped Kent would be able to answer before they left. However, in the few moments between Kent's arrival and their departure for Porvenir the following morning, he found little time left for discussion. Another blemish to his plans, but there was still the drive out to the house; they could talk then. As they climbed into the car and headed out of town, Kent casually told him that they would be picking up the relative and her baby for the drive to El Porvenir. She apparently had no form of transportation of her own. Time was ticking away; Ordin felt a strong need to talk to Kenton and put things in order. All of his efforts to fit everything into a limited space were conflicting with Honduran time, which appeared even more casual than Hawaiian time. Nonetheless, somewhere near the appointed hour, give or take sixty minutes, they arrived at the town of El Porvenir.

His drive through the little town had been interesting. The quiet beach town had once been a busy community during the height of the fruit plantation days; it was actually a seat of commerce before La Ceiba was constructed. There still were pineapple fields but most of the bigger industry was gone. Porvenir was a beach community and people from all around the area loved to go there to recreate or vacation. Kent had mentioned, after his own inspection, that the house was in a Honduran neighborhood, which meant that we would have an opportunity to learn about the culture and traditions of these people. When we moved to Hawai'i, we had chosen not to move to a gated community of "ha'oles" from the mainland. There is no sense in exploring new areas to live in if we were going to take our old habits and beliefs with us. Mark Twain once said, "Travel is the death of bigotry.", but those words lose their truthfulness if we remain shrouded by our old ways when we travel away from home. Another adage is that you never really know a person until you live with them, and this house was going to give us just that opportunity.

A gravel road led through the town, bedded with local river rock. The colorful, smooth shapes of the stones challenged the tires to stay on track, while the rocking and swaying auto groaned to maintain balance. The weight of daily traffic easily slid the stones to form deep ruts, similar to driving over a roadbed of various-sized marbles. The assortment of houses along the byways ranged from modest dwellings of vintage timber or block to homes that reflected greater affluence. Unfinished construction, ghosts of a time of greater prosperity, and newer concrete structures influenced by the Spanish architecture joined the neighborhood in an array of colors that ranged from raw cement to painted colors of pink, green, yellow and turquoise. Horses roam the town freely—perhaps the highway department's answer to roadside vegetation problems. A new city hall building and a social center suggested a growing interest in the community's identity. Many *Pulperias* (family-owned, mini-convenience stores) dotted the neighborhood, hinting at a level of economic vitality; yet personal car traffic was rare enough that any unknown automobile received prolonged scrutiny. These were the impressions that Ordin had as he rode through the town, his mind questioning, "What would Malana think?" He had little time to pursue the issue since the car had stopped outside large, terra-cotta colored, metal gates. Ordin finally stood outside the gates of his possible casa.

The heavy latch lifted and the caretaker swung the gateway open to allow them access. Here stood the house that Ordin had seen only in photos on the web. The sensation for him must have been similar to coming face-to-face with a mail-order bride. The large, yellow, two-story house sat at the front of the three-quarter-acre property, with almost half of its base square footage used as a carport/patio under the twenty-five-hundred square-foot upper story. The write-up on the web claimed a laundry room, and two bedrooms with baths downstairs. Friends of ours were considering moving into the downstairs and possibly adding a studio apartment, using some of the carport area. On inspection, Ordin found the downstairs designed as living quarters for domestic help. It would need extensive remodeling to bring it up to the standards of our westernized friends. This was a disappointment, yet he realized that much of the distress he felt was caused, in part, by his eyes not seeing the picture that his mind had already created.

The climb to the second story brought Ordin to the open veranda that bordered two sides of the house to allow a full view of the *Pico Bonito* Mountain. *Bonito* means beautiful, and its magnificent peak was striking as Ordin gazed over the terrain in the late morning sun. Turning east, his eyes scanned the lush, verdant yard dotted with young fruit trees. His eyes searched for the river pictured on the internet advertisement; disappointment number two: it was hidden behind the eight-foot privacy wall. As he was processing each piece of information, an automobile at the gate began honking its horn. The caretaker, recognizing the auto, again pulled wide the entry to allow access for the carload of out-of-town relatives who were coming to weekend at the beach. The yard began to fill and the stairway became packed with Hondurans of all ages and sizes. As the throng took over the house, our hero could feel his high standards for home inspection carried away on the soft Caribbean breezes and gently whisked out to sea. Amid dogs, children, caretaker and reconnecting family members, Ordin set about performing his task. His singularly focused mind besieged by the swarm of unfamiliar language surrounding him as the group inquisitively followed him throughout the house. Shaking his head, he could see many of the rules he used to govern his life discarded at the immigration station. There was no place for them in Honduras.

SECTION II

The Journey

Adios and Aloha

It was finally happening. As I awakened, the sensation washed over me that "This will be the last time." Pueo's soft voice was insisting that it was time for our morning routine. As I stood to follow her, there it was again: "This will be the last time." This will be the last time I walk in the darkness of the Hawaiian predawn, smelling the sweet scent of Jasmine and Forbidden Fruit of India as their fragrance hangs in the morning stillness. This will be the last time that I walk the familiar rolling contours of the acre that my friend Flo, Ordin, and I cleared, filled, and planted. It was also the last time that I had to hear those noxious little Coqui frogs that had invaded our island. My mind began running through the checklist of all that had been done, and what still needed to be done before we left for the airport at noon.

When I was investigating choices on how to ship our possessions, I had an impression that we were to take only ten boxes on this move. I thought we had downsized a lot when we moved to Hawai'i five years before, but ten boxes! I was sure the universe was not being literal so I fudged and we shipped fifteen to the freight forwarder who would send them on to Honduras. Before we left the mainland we had given antiques and family pieces to our children. Friends helped us with a yard sale to get rid of the rest, but stuff seems drawn to folks like dust to glass and here we were, after just a few short years, with a houseful again. My friend, Flo, was taking most of the furniture pieces but she would leave them at the house until we were gone so there would be something to sleep on and eat at up to the last minute. It pleased me to know that she would have the things I had loved having about me. This move helped me realize that it never hurts to part with things you love if you give them to the people you love, so that is what we did. We sorted every item we owned into one of four piles: one to ship, one to send to children, one to leave as aloha with friends, and one for a sale. Everything else was trash.

I had figured the shipping would cost us about one hundred dollars a box, and the boxes needed to be under forty-five pounds. I was mailing them by parcel post to a freight forwarder who would send them on for another seventy cents a pound. It was an interesting study to see what items earned that value. One friend told me that this move was a rebirthing for us and, just as we came into the first birth with nothing, we needed to consider a similar action for this one. I did my best but I was sure that when I unpacked my chosen treasures in Honduras, it would be a repeat of the unpacking in Hawai'i. I would wonder, "What was I thinking when I packed this!"

Our cat was a major concern. As traumatic as it was going to be for us to take our four-year-old Pu five thousand miles from the only home she had known, we felt it would be far worse to leave her with someone who might treat her like...a cat. After all, she is family; just a family member with a tail. She had been away from home only once in her life and that was when she went for spaying. Having survived that ordeal, she has never felt the need to travel again. It was not too difficult to get her comfortable with being in her new carrier, since she has always felt that anything new coming into the house was for her. However, once we began the acclimating of her to car travel, the challenge began. She told us, in no uncertain terms, that she was not happy with that state of affairs. Now we were at the time when a health certificate was needed to travel by plane. That would require another trip to a vet. I dreaded the feeling of betrayal I would be aware of by the end of that appointment.

Procrastination was sparing my nerves; I kept putting off the time to call for the appointment as long as I could. Subsequently, a miracle occurred. One day I picked up an old copy of an island newspaper to use for packing and, as I opened to the center, an ad stood out: "Kindred Spirits, veterinary service." Fate had stepped in to save me again but this time with a vet who had feline savvy AND made house calls.

Dr. Shannon was a tiny young woman with purple streaks in her hair. She kicked off her shoes at the door, walked across the room, sat cross-legged on the wood floor and spread out her paperwork in front of her. She interviewed me for the important details needed while Pueo examined her. In no time at all Pueo and I were as comfortable as Dr. Shannon appeared to be. There was very little protest from Pu as she was gently examined, or as she later received her shot. This amazing vet even stayed for an hour afterwards to make sure that our feline had no adverse reaction to the immunization. During the hour, the doctor discussed ways to help remove stress for Pu during the trip…which meant for us as well. Our original thought had been to keep her in the plane with us for each leg of the journey, but our chosen airline had a policy of not allowing animals in-cabin for long flights. They instead have designed a special insulated "safe room" with an attendant. In conceding to the regulations, I realized that this was a blessing in disguise.

There was another concern: our file cabinet. It was the job neither of us wanted. Years on years of files and papers, haunting us like the spirit of Christmas past, carried our history from Florida and were waiting to disturb our plans for the future. "I refuse to take all of that into Honduras!" I told Ordin. "Most of it is yours; you go through it." Each of us wanted the other to take on the task. Days turned into weeks; the ominous, lateral, double-drawer cabinet sternly waited in our office, defying us to remove a shred of paper. It was beginning to seem hopeless. We had given the cabinet to a friend but we could not send old client and business information with it. What is more, the files were NOT on my list of valuables to ship at one hundred dollars a box.

As we were approaching the last ten days, we came on a brilliant plan. Rather than burn out a shredder or our nerves, we dug through the cabinet to create an "Important File." This contained our birth and marriage certificates, diplomas, licenses, passports and such. Next, we added copies of e-mail correspondences about the house, Pueo's health certificates and our airline tickets. All this went into a waterproof envelope that we could carry with us. Out of the blue, there was a light at the end of the tunnel. Our feeling of dread began to rise to one of hope as an empty space became prominent in the first drawer. Next, we boxed up three years of tax returns, and anything we felt was relevant to business interest in the new home; the space in the drawers was growing. Once we had removed all that was necessary, we started eliminating our paper trail with a fire ritual. For three evenings in a row, we dragged lawn chairs, beer and a CD player with selected music to an old fire barrel set in the back of the property. We filled the barrel with records, files and receipts, sprinkled them with a light covering of charcoal lighter fluid and then applied a match. The burst of flame brought an immediate sense of relief, freeing us from the past by cremating the remnants of old thoughts, beliefs and perceptions. We watched the sparks and smoke offer bits and pieces of old worries, struggles and pain to the four directions, while we shared our dreams of the future. When the last drawer emptied and the final remnant of paper burned, we both agreed the job we each dreaded most became the one that we enjoyed most.

We were not sure what to do about our mail. With the amount of new construction going on, our rural mailboxes were at a premium and the new owner of our house was concerned there might not be one for him when he moved in. I was not sure if my bank was willing to send my statement through the mail to Central America and there was always a chance we might decide not to stay. We did a little research and found we could rent a Post Net box for a year, with directions to send our mail twice a month. This let the property owner add his name to our rural delivery box, and we later forwarded ours to the new box. We asked Kent to procure for us a post office box in La Ceiba and gave this address to our family and friends. I had heard that mail delivery in Honduras was slow and not very reliable, so it seemed best to test this with personal mail first. So far, I find this information outdated; the mail service seems a bit slow but reliable. Either way, when we left, most of our personal business was confined to one credit card that I could pay online, our bank statements and a life insurance premium that came three times a year. If there was something I neglected, it would show up in the mail.

During our last seven years in Florida, we operated a natural health clinic which we had planned to sell before moving. What we were not sure of was how soon to place it with an agent. As it ended, when we did list it, the time was too short to find a qualified, knowledgeable, and interested buyer. It was heartbreaking to spend years building something, only to lock the doors for the last time and simply walk away, but we were fortunate to have three clients who had, over time, become students and then experienced apprentices. Now it was time for Ordin to sell his inspection business and we did not want history to repeat itself. He had developed this small, independent, home inspection company as a part-time business but the reliability and quality of his assessments had built a reputation with customers and real estate agents in our area. Offers had come from other inspectors wanting to assume his contacts but they were not willing to pay his business price. He felt a heavy sense of responsibility to pending clients and repeat customers; integrity and honesty were essential.

We were into our last forty-five days and O worried that time to train a buyer was draining away. He had wanted thirty days to train and help a buyer make a smooth transition but we were rapidly approaching that final window of time. His distress over the situation was interfering with his ability to make other rational decisions, so he decided to take a drive to the ocean. He felt the salt air would clear the congestion of worry from his brain. When he returned two hours later, his face appeared more relaxed and he had the look of someone on a mission. After a quick stop at the refrigerator for something cold to drink and a cool-lipped kiss on the cheek for me, he disappeared down the hall, heading for his office. He was turning to enter the doorway when I heard him yell that he would call me when he had something to show me.

I was deep into newspaper and boxes when I heard his voice. It had been almost two hours since he had vanished into his hallowed chamber to work on the solution to his problem. As I made the short trip down the hall of our little plantation home, I could hear Ordin humming and rustling paper; a good sign. The first thing I noticed as I entered the compact room was the "artistic clutter" of papers about the floor, but O redirected my attention to the computer-printed photos hanging on the door and adorning the shelf over his desk. One of the photos showed an image of him shaking hands with an unknown person while handing over the keys to the business truck. The second picture was a computer-generated check, payable to Ordin, for the total amount he was asking for his business. He planned to spend time looking at these each day, while his mind surrendered to that new reality.

This was a concept we had learned years before, but as often happens when the human mind is offered a choice between productive tranquility and destructive havoc, it will cast aside its creative tools for the adrenaline response of stress. Ordin followed his plan; the pictures were left hanging and he spent time with them each day. Then, just as so many other things had happened for us, within a week the phone rang. A husband and wife were looking for an in-home business; they were island people, well-known and respected in the community. They owned rental property so he was already familiar with troubleshooting problems, plus he had construction ability and she had office skills. They were a perfect team to pass on the small company to. One more task moved to the completed list.

Now came the hardest part: saying good-bye to my friend, Flo. Our shared friendship had been the answer to both of our prayers. While I was still in Florida, in preparation for making the move to Hawai'i, I had prayed for a friend...a Hawaiian friend who could teach me the essence of the islands. Meanwhile Flo, in Hilo, had recently lost her mother to cancer and then, shortly afterwards, her heart was again torn in grief from the death of a beloved friend. The void that remained caused an ache that she wanted healed; she prayed for a friend.

I knew her the moment I saw her, just an hour after we landed in Hilo. She had been in my dreams for the last month before we left the mainland. I was never able to see her face...only her form...and I could see her grown children in the background, suggesting to me that they would always be in contact but not closely involved with us, busy with their own lives.

Flo was head of housekeeping for the complex where we had reservations to stay. Since we were arriving after business hours, she had volunteered to hang around after work to make sure we could locate our apartment. She was a sturdy Hawaiian woman with her feet well planted on the ground, her thick, black hair pulled back in a ponytail. She smelled a little of beer, a bit of cigarette smoke and the perspiration of a day's work, but those were only tiny things about her; her great big smile, enormous bear hug and Aloha spirit matched her form and the size of her heart. Even though I was sure she was my gift, Flo was far from what I expected. When I prayed for a friend who could teach me the essence of the islands, I thought I would find someone who would teach me the mysteries of the culture. Through my friendship with Flo, I found the true essence of the islands is the spirit of Aloha.

She and I had become joined at the hip for the five years O and I were there. I met all of her family and she had traveled with me to the mainland and met mine. I was there to support her through her job change and the loss of her spouse; she was at my side when my brother, and later my mother, passed away. Other than during her work hours, where one of us was, so was the other. She spent all of her holidays and weekends with us, and now we were going to say good-bye.

When O and I were certain we would leave the island and were relatively sure that it would be to Honduras, I had to break the news to Flo. As much as neither Flo nor I wanted it to happen, each of us had the deep understanding that, to fulfill our destinies, this time of separation had to come. Even as we began to understand this, it was a reality that neither of us wanted to accept, so Flo and I began to set up a plan where she could take vacation time and travel with us. She could help Ordin and I make the move to Honduras. In that way she could be the first to see our new home and share the experience, and the initial separation would not seem so abrupt. She applied for her passport and was waiting to learn our departure dates so she could apply for her time off when Ordin's inspection brought the disappointing news: the house conditions would be a little rough at first for a guest. Flo was truly an island gal, having been born and raised on The Big Island. She would have walked across hot lava for me, but going into a foreign country without knowing whether she would have a bed to sleep in...that was asking a bit much. She agreed to wait until we settled in so her visit could be a shared adventure, not a horror story. But this decision was easier to make than to follow through.

Flo had taken the last four days off from work and had been camping on the futon in the living room, helping out where she could. She planned to say her goodbyes at the house, then stay to close it up for us. I knew her heart was breaking; I could feel the same tightness in my chest. I was concerned about leaving her to be alone once we pulled out of the drive, so I asked a mutual friend to come by just before we would leave. This would allow Flo to say good-bye the way she wanted, but would keep her from being alone those first few hours. As we stowed the bags in the car, Flo and I looked at each other; this was the moment. Now the words would finally need to be said. Neither of us wanted to acknowledge the tears of the other. We held each other, dreading the next few moments which would separate us for an unknown time. We kissed each other's wet checks and then performed the most sacred of Hawaiian rituals: we exchanged breath. With this rite, she was forever part of me, and I of her. It was no longer good-bye; it was Aloha a hui hou...our hearts connected until we meet again.

Come Fly with Me

Neither Ordin nor I have much experience at foreign travel. Customs Agents and Immigration Officials are foreign enough for us, so Ordin came up with a plan to minimize customs inspections by taking everything we needed as carry-on, but this also restricted our luggage to the barest essentials. The new house had only sparse furnishings and no linens, and it would be at least a week or so before the first of our parcels arrived. Therefore, one of our four carry-on would need to include two towels, toiletries, our bed sheets and whatever clothing could be contained in the remaining two bags which airline regulations limited in size and weight. The weight limit was not too great a factor since the size of the bags allowed as carry-on would have required rocks or gold to exceed the weight restrictions. Add to this picture that another one of our carryon items was a ten-pound cat, and the image of refugees fleeing across the border begins to form. We knew there was a washing machine in the laundry under the house and, if it worked, it would allow us to stretch our wardrobe. However, the remaining two bags containing our personal items would still need packing with all the expertise of a seasoned flight attendant. Nevertheless, we hoped that keeping ourselves minimized would help reduce attention as we carried Pueo into country.

As carefully as our vet had coached us and done her research, she did not discover any restrictions for taking animals into Honduras, so we did not know what to expect. This could make things very easy for us, or become our worst nightmare. We had complied with Continental Airlines health requirements and hoped Pueo's U.S.D.A. certificate, with its official embossed seal, would be enough to impress Honduran Immigration officials. Our friend, Oscar, had already flown to Honduras to deal with personal business and was timing his trip so he would be in country to help us make our transition. He had stopped to see our lawyer in the capital and planned to meet us when we landed in San Pedro Sula. Everything was going smoothly until we got his call the night before we were to board the plane. It seemed the lawyer had just informed him of regulations which required that a Honduran veterinarian be willing to take responsibility for Pueo when we arrived. We were well past the turn-back point; all we could say to him at that moment was, "Whatever it takes, please take care of it."

I have come to believe that traveling with four-footed family members is actually more stressful for the two-footed members who accompany them. I remember the night my husband made the phone reservations for Pueo's flight. We had chosen the most direct route possible with the fewest hours of travel. As I had mentioned earlier, our overprotective plan was to keep her by our side all the way from Hilo to Honduras. Aloha Airlines had no problem with the plan as long as we had the correct size carrier and arrived at the airport three hours early. Since only three animals are allowed to fly in-cabin, they are chosen on a first-come basis. Our anxiety set in after learning the Continental folks could not conform to our plan. They explained to us that their policy did not allow animals in the cabin on overseas flights. This was not the impression we received from information that another agent had told us when we first started researching this journey, so we were stunned and alarmed. Ordin's reaction, due to the change in our plans and Pueo's possible trauma, offered interesting insight about why pets and their owners need to be separated for long journeys. The agent tried to explain to Ordin that animals were constantly attended to in an insulated "safe area" under the main cabin and that our cat would be secure. I could hear the distress in O's voice, mirroring my own feelings, as I listened to him set up the reservations for Pu. Yet, as I became aware of our state of unease, a sense of calm occurred; a knowing that this really was the best for all of us.

Our next concern was for the final leg of the flight. Our on-line research pointed out that all animals had to enter Central America in-cabin. That meant we were going to need to take along the soft-sided carrier that Pueo would use in her trip from Hilo to Honolulu. Once we landed in Honolulu, we would have three hours to soothe the nerves of our furry travel companion and then get her accustomed to her larger, hard-sided carrier. This would be her "coach seat" down in the cargo space while the rest of us slept above. I had already planned to place a drop of lavender oil under the pad in her carrier and a drop of a homeopathic remedy for distress on her tongue...I was hoping that Ordin and I would not need the same. Once across the ocean to Houston, we would need to claim our feline from cargo and slip her back into the soft carrier for the final flight into Honduras. The itinerary gave us one hour to make this switch and, according to the Continental agent on the phone, it could be done.

The day of travel went well. Pueo was a trooper, protesting only a bit about traveling in the car, but when we did not turn around and return to the house; she decided to see what would happen next. All through the three-hour wait at Hilo airport she seemed content to be safely contained at our feet, hiding behind the blue mesh wall of her carrier, watching the comings and goings of numerous sets of ankles. The homeopathic remedy did its job later as we waited to board the small plane to Oahu; across the gate from a couple of cats that were objecting to travel. Ordin and I were like proud parents with our little girl, traveling like a professional, as we landed in Honolulu and began the search for the cargo terminal where we would transfer her to the larger carrier and surrender her to the care of attendants. This was the last we would see of her until we claimed her after the all-night flight to Houston.

The gate where we landed in Houston was just across the hall from the one taking us to Honduras. When we asked for our feline, they informed us that the cargo area where we would need to pick her up was in a completely different terminal. We had only an hour to make our next flight. I am sure we set an Olympic world record dashing from one end of Terminal E to the other end of Terminal C, Pueo's papers, soft-sided carrier and our carry-on bags in hand. We were gasping for oxygen as we arrived at the freight office desk. The bone-dry condition of our throats made it impossible to do more than croak as we waved our animal flight receipt at the two men who answered the bell on the cargo room door. Their sense of urgency was not as great as our own as they disappeared once more behind the DO NOT ENTER sign on the cargo room door. We waited...precious minutes racing by...when I finally decided to enter the forbidden zone myself. The two men looked up from their discussion, but Pueo saw us and we saw her. Ordin brandished the papers at them and showed ID as I removed Pu from her large container, holding her tight and cooing her name, then gently transferred her to her small blue tote. Our family intact again, we started the run back to our terminal and the security checkpoint. Part of security procedure was to remove Pueo from her carrier, and quickly but without a sense of alarm carry her to the other side, and then coax her back into her carrier. This completed, we were free to sprint for our gate. My stamina amazed me as I ran the inclined hallway and the degree of agility I summoned as I sprang down the motorized walkway, but for all of our effort...the waiting room was empty at Gate Nine. Breathless, we watched our plane pull away from the ramp.

The Continental service desk personnel at the Houston airport were very sympathetic to our problem and could not understand who would have given us all this misinformation. According to them, Miss Pu could have traveled through to San Pedro Sula in the safe area or, if notified that she was being retrieved in Houston, could have been held in "safe keep" at the arriving terminal. As we tried to recover our breath, becoming educated in animal travel rules was the least of our interests. It was ten o'clock in the morning, we had not slept or eaten for hours, we were distressed about our missed flight and aggravated about the perplexing information. Our efforts to stay calm must have appeared weak since the service desk personnel abruptly stopped the discourse, arranged a discounted room rate at a local hotel and issued new tickets for the following morning. As the three of us stood on the curbside awaiting the shuttle, our adrenal response wearing off, an overwhelming sense of fatigue washed over me and I was ready to find my bed.

After seventeen hours confinement in carriers, we knew Pueo was going to need to stretch. She seemed calm enough as we transported her around the airport and hotel, protesting only twice while doing the "security shuffle," but the drop of lavender oil under the pad in her carrier had helped keep our timid traveler relaxed. For a non-traveling kitty, she had acted like a seasoned pro. As the hotel room door closed behind us, our first concern was to her comfort. We unzipped the carrier to allow her access to the room. Tentatively, she peeked and then crept from the place that had kept her safe to enter this environment of new smells, sounds and shapes. In her home, the small space under our bed had always been her safe place. As her eyes recognized the shape of a bed in the room, she moved quickly to it. It tore at my heart to watch this act of survival, so I dug her out of her cubbyhole, wrapped her into my shirt and held her against my heart.

As I sat holding her, I silently asked a blessing on all of us. Then I started softly singing the special song that I had sung for her since she was a kitten. It was the song that would let her know that I was close when she went into the deep jungle, when the thunder would roll or when she would be frightened. It was "our" song and a sound of safety to her. After a half hour, her trembling had finally eased and she was ready to come out of my shirt. We drank some water, had a bite to eat and then crawled into bed together. A makeshift litter box was waiting if she overcame her dehydration. The day may not have started to my liking, but when it was through I knew this break in traveling had been a blessing.

At nine o'clock in the morning, we were back at the airport to try again. This time our small family was together. As we waited for our boarding passes, the ticketing agent informed us that our carry-on bags were now too large and would need to be checked. Our plans were foiled again, but this time I was pleased. My preference has always been to check bags when I travel but, because of our cat and customs and other unknowns, I had surrendered my liking to the wisdom of my partner. All these carry-on bags had me feeling like a desert nomad, hauling our life's necessities around. This change left us free to carry only my tote bag and Miss Pu. We settled into the airport lounge chairs with thirty minutes to await boarding. We were in good spirits and looking forward to the end of the journey, when suddenly, we heard our names called over the intercom. Apprehension took hold as I immediately went to the service desk to deal with the next challenge, but dread became delight as new boarding passes printed out. Our economy seats were upgraded to first class...compensation for the problems of the day before. It was only a two-and-a-half hour flight but we would enter C.A. in style!

After we boarded the plane and settled into our seats, the flight attendants brought beverages and breakfast. Pueo, in her carrier, settled at our feet. We plugged in the earphones for the movie and dropped the shade; all three of us fell asleep from nervous exhaustion. An announcement of our approach to San Pedro Sula airport woke me and I opened the window shade in time to see us dropping into solid gray clouds. It was an eerie sight having a wall of solid stillness pressing against the windows. Our pilot attempted his approach three times before he announced to the cabin that he could not land and we would head to San Salvador to wait for weather improvements. San Salvador? Isn't that in El Salvador? Oh, my gosh! Uneasiness swept over me that brought on images of hijacking. My knowledge of El Salvador limited to, and tainted by, the drama movies of espionage, corruption and drug- related violence that were marketed for U.S consumption over the last twenty years. I had to pull myself together. This was a U.S. plane; I had seen the weather was bad. I am sure my eyes were large but I calmed my breathing to steady my pulse.

Our two-and-a-half-hour flight ended having a five-hour layover before we returned to our point of departure—Houston. I added our first-class bump to my list of gratitude as our plane waited on the edge of the runway in San Salvador. The local ground crew serviced the plane as the flight attendants served beverages inside the plane. The flight attendants did their best to keep passengers as comfortable as possible, considering the circumstances. When the flight crew received their instructions to return to Houston, the passengers had consumed all the liquids inside the craft. Ordin spent some time talking to a missionary who was returning to the La Ceiba area and learned this was a common occurrence during the rainy season. During this time our little Pu had not made a sound, but it was her habit to hide quietly when worried. I was a little surprised that she had continued her silence during so many hours of being on the ground, so I opened her bag to stroke and talk to her. She was not responding. Her eyes were open but she did not try to stand. We had not offered her water, knowing she would not drink while in this strange environment, and now I became alarmed.

Our flight attendant saw my concern and recounted how her cat had dehydrated on a plane once and needed intravenous treatment; panic and guilt flooded over me. I dipped my finger in water and forced Pueo's mouth open to dampen her teeth and tongue. I placed a drop on her lips, hoping that she would lick it off. I moistened her head with a damp tissue and I prayed. When the plane landed in Houston, I was a woman with a mission. I wanted to get my cat out of her carrier, let her stretch and have water. I wanted her to have a chance to restore herself. Clearly, the U.S. officials in Houston were not aware of my mission.

Our ten-hour confinement did not end when we disembarked as we had to go through immigration. Technically, since we had not come from outside the country, we could not go through general public processing. We stood in a line, like prisoners, for an hour while immigration officers tried to figure out what to do with us. Finally, we were processed and then herded to the Continental service desk where a detached young woman stamped certificates, issued new tickets and instructed us to stand in yet another line to await a bus to a hotel. To me, it was imperative that we get Pu out of her carrier. I was through with lines. I was like a lioness protecting her cub. Ordin fielded the crowd; a U-turn moved us out of the masses and into the airport hotel. There would be no more lines for our princess; she got her first-class treatment at the Marriott.

We later realized that Pu's lack of response was her natural way of dealing with an unnatural situation. Once we quietly locked ourselves away inside our room, I sat and held Pu as I had done the day before. This time the routine was not as new. She recovered herself in half the time, timidly starting to explore the room and having some nourishment. After a short time, the three of us crawled into the fluffy, king-size bed to get some rest; we had an early flight tomorrow. Before settling into bed I had pulled the drapes open slightly on the floor-to-ceiling windows of our room to offer Pueo something of interest to watch. Twice, during the night, I had found her off the bed and seated at the window, studying the minuscule world of lights and movement below her tenth-floor observation booth. I am sure she knew she was not in the jungles of Hawai'i anymore.

At seven the next morning we were seated on the plane and ready for takeoff. This was not the usual morning flight to San Pedro Sula. It had been put together to complete the itinerary from the day before without interfering with the current day's schedule. Since this was an unusual time and we had not been able to call, there was the possibility there would be no one at San Pedro Sula to meet us. Our friend, Oscar, had planned to be at the gate with the necessary papers for our kitty's entrance the first day, as was the van driver who would take us all on the three-hour drive to El Porvenir. They would have learned of our missed flight and arranged to be there the second day, but would anyone know about this early schedule on the third day? Another stress filled situation. I do not believe our level of anxiety ever lessened throughout the journey, since we always had a new crisis to attend to.

Aside from the fact that none of our travel was going according to plan, the trip went quite smoothly. After we landed in San Pedro Sula, we did our best to keep Pueo in as low a profile as possible while we worked our way through the immigration line. Our efforts to keep her out of sight were challenged by the bright blue, mesh carrier she was riding in but, nonetheless, I held the thought of being invisible and she cooperated with her silent study of the officials as we went through the process of arrival. Once our passports were stamped, it was time to locate our luggage and deal with the last potential barrier of getting Pueo "in country": the Customs officials. The baggage claim area was a confusion of people, luggage and languages as we waited for the carousel to begin its laborious effort. Ordin and I were as nervous as Pu, each of us craving invisibility, when, out of the blue, a short, stocky man wearing an ear-to-ear smile was standing between us. His nametag identified him as a baggage handler named Dennis and his greeting revealed a fair degree of multi-language skill. As soon as he confirmed that we wanted assistance, he tucked us under his protective wing, quickly gathered our bags and then whisked us to the head of the line at the security checkpoint. We were moving through the process with amazing speed until officers began insisting that we place our small, blue tote bag through the security X-ray. With each refusal we repeated the phrase "*el gato*" in our English-sounding Spanish. Dennis disappeared for only a minute while this fiasco took place and returned with a young man in uniform. The young officer escorted us away from the crowd and into an office near the rear of the baggage area. He directed us to sit in front of a desk while he went through piles of papers in the rear of the room. My mind kept offering images of horrible possibilities as we found ourselves caught in the exact situation we had worked so hard to avoid. We had wanted to become invisible to move our cat safely through customs and we had now been singled out of the crowd, awaiting the outcome.

The young man returned to the desk where we had been left seated, and slid a sheet of paper in front of me pointing to where he wanted me to sign. The first thing I noticed on the paper was the official seal of Honduras. As my heart stepped up yet another rate, I tried to understand the two paragraphs of printed, Spanish words that were just above the line that awaited my signature. What did this all mean? Would they take Pueo from us? Were they going to let us pass? Would they require quarantine? Thankfully, Dennis and his competent English had remained with us so I passed the official-looking letter to him to decipher. As he scanned the paper, my eyes never left his face. Intently, I studied it for some sign of meaning or emotion. Within a few quick moments his face broke into the now-familiar, ear-to-ear grin. He laid the paper on the desk in front of me, his finger pressed to the word "*Gato*". He then began pointing out other familiar words that my frightened eyes had missed, such as Pueo's name and mine where they were buried in the Spanish jargon. The final item that he pointed out was the seal and signature of a veterinarian to the left of where I was to sign my name. It was much later when we learned the story of Oscar and the veterinarian waiting to meet us at the airport on the day we were first due to arrive. On the second day, when the weather had interfered with our landing, Oscar was waiting for us without the vet but with the official papers. Not knowing what else to do, Oscar decided to leave the paperwork with the receiving office in case we came in later that day or in case something interfered with our arrival on the third day...which it did.

We had no way to notify Oscar of the special flight that had been scheduled for us on the next day; we hoped he would think to ask. We were not even sure if the driver who planned to pick us up would know about the problem and check for plane schedules and know we had arrived in San Pedro Sula two hours before the regularly scheduled flight. Ordin and I kept a constant lookout for Oscar as we went through the customs and immigration area, hoping to see his smiling face in the crowd outside the door. Yet, unknown to us, as we were being processed at the airport, Oscar was leisurely enjoying breakfast at a nearby hotel.

In the throng of people, nothing seemed familiar to me; it was a heady feeling, like being caught in water current. I had a tight grip on Ordin's travel vest with one hand as I pulled one piece of our luggage with the other. He had Pueo in her carrier slung under one arm and had stacked the remaining two pieces of luggage on top of each other. Eyes focused on the parking lot, he pushed forward like a tugboat, maneuvering us through the harbor of traveling people. He stopped only once and that was to throw words over his shoulder, of which all I caught was "driver," but it was enough. My eyes began to search over the heads of people in the direction of his intensity. Then, among the crowd of people waiting outside the gate, I saw our driver. Thankfully, he and his copilot had learned of the schedule change and returned to wait for us. The driver was waving his arms for attention while his assistant had a sign, with the printed letters "O R D I N", held upside down in his hands. For the moment, we had a respite from anxiety. We had arrived.

SECTION III

Our Honduras Home

Week One

Becoming One

My mind awakened as I felt the coolness of Pueo's paw hesitantly touch my arm. "Come be with me in the quiet." her soft manner spoke to me. It was our time. Sometimes we shared it with Ordin, but never anyone else. I turned my head, looking for his form beside me in the indigo light of morning. The smoky blue silhouette of the mountains beyond drew my gaze and gently reminded me: this is my new home. Pu's insistence broke the moment and I slipped into my mother's old flannel shirt to walk the depth of the house and go down the stairs into the yard. The shirt had been my choice when she asked what I wanted for my birthday just 3 months before she passed away. Wearing it was comforting and gave me the feeling that she was near.

Roosters had started to crow. Well, that was no different from Hawai'i. The yard had many of the scents I was accustomed to, but the manicured setting within the courtyard was a drastic change from the barely controlled jungle we were used to. This was our first morning at the new place and Pu's first venture outside the house since we had arrived. She crouched on the floor of the gazebo, acting as sentry while I secured the yard. I was hoping the familiarity of routine would offer her a feeling of stability. She and I had established this ritual after wild pigs invaded our backyard in Hawai'i. With that morning task completed, I performed my personal ritual: filling my lungs with the breath of the four directions and softly offering the chant taught to me by the Kupuna on the island. It was the way of the old ones, asking for guidance and to be accepted by the land. Pueo barely tolerates my chanting, but she knows that when it ends we will walk the damp grass together and explore the mysteries of the gardens. As we moved around the perimeter of the yard, from one perfectly pruned planting to another, my mind kept drawing comparisons, judging about the decision we had made in coming here. Visiting a third world country is much different from seeing it as your home.

The poor conditions of the highways, police checkpoints and poorly disposed-of rubbish were the first items I was aware of as we had traveled from the airport at San Pedro Sula. I knew Ordin hoped I was pleased and so I made a point to shift my perspective to the natural beauty of the countryside as we traveled the coastal highway toward La Ceiba. After all, I thought, we are still miles away from the location of our home. I surrendered my scrutiny and allowed myself to relax and become interested as the van navigated past the horse drawn carts and potholes scattered along the way. The warm breeze flowing through the open windows was a welcome change from the climate-controlled environments that had confined us over the last few days. My dehydrated skin had been begging for the moister air it was accustomed to from island life. At least here it could breathe again.

Gazing out the windows, I could see lush vegetation, palm nut groves and, occasionally, the ocean beyond. There were fields fenced with barbwire strung between lengths of young tree trunks. This species of tree and proper climate had caused many of the "posts" to begin growing again, a minor distraction from the scenery. The driver maneuvered the van with practiced skill past the two-wheeled horse carts hauling bananas or pineapples and general foot traffic that shared the thoroughfare. I found myself relaxing as I watched the local women carrying produce in plastic containers expertly balanced on their heads and children playing in the yards along the road. All the while, I listened to Ordin's commentary, reporting on insights he had gleaned from Oscar and José when he made this same journey just four months before. All I was seeing around me reflected the quiet lifestyle we had hoped to find.

As we neared La Ceiba, I sat forward in my seat, anticipating a sign that would signal the turn to our small community: *El Porvenir* (the future). Well, it was to be my future. A sign pointed to a hardtop road that divided pineapple fields and then disappeared over a small rise as it approached a single-lane, wooden bridge. The narrow bridge had parallel timber thrown loosely on crossbeam supports. The sight of those wooden planks prompted my mind to begin calculating our chances as the distance to the bridge closed. Luckily, I avoided the embarrassing moment of cautioning our driver when I noticed a three-quarter-ton field truck awaiting its turn to cross from the other side. Our speed never wavered as we approached the bridge; the large timbers grumbled under the weight of the van, and a moment later, our front tires had grabbed the roadway on the other side. As we performed our feat of daring, our driver honked to the waiting truck as though to say, "We made it; good luck to you, too." The smiles and waves coming from the field crew in the back of the truck shared in celebrating our accomplishment. This incident and a stand of beautiful Rainbow Eucalyptus trees were our welcome to Porvenir.

We followed the hardtop as it made a right turn, heading for the center of the little beach town. Now the journey took on a new interest for me; this was my new neighborhood. I watched with curiosity the different aspects of life offered for view as the road approached a bend. We had already passed a small vending stand under the trees alongside the road where a woman hand squeezed fresh sugarcane to sell for juice. Three children were sitting astride a horse, headed for the beach with their inner tube in their hands, while just beyond, two small pigs raced each other along the ditch line. These pleasurable experiences reinforced the images I had created of living here. Soon the pavement ended and we were traveling on a dusty gravel side road. No...this was not a side road! It was the main thoroughfare of town! The dust and road conditions called for reducing our speed. We slowly moved along the road, dodging large rocks and potholes. It amazed me to watch bike riders maneuver their way over the rocky road, carrying passengers poised perfectly, keeping their erect balance around every twist and curve. This was a practiced skill.

It was the lunch hour as we made our journey through town; many folks had gathered on porches or in yards under shade trees, sharing food and conversation. Laundry hung across shrubs and fences to dry in the sun. The fine film of dust everywhere heightened the disparaging look of many the buildings. I was also aware of the number of lean dogs that roamed the town and it told me that Pueo would never see the outside of our walled yard. That dream, with other misconceptions, fell away among the rubble in the road as we traveled the last few yards to our front gate. I hardly realized we had arrived; I was still numbly processing the dust, the dogs and the shabby homes. Ordin had pointed out the new City Hall building, the large social center and soccer field. Every yard had beautiful flowering shrubs and fruit trees but my mind still clung to the images of poverty. Pueo might not be the only one who never left the walls of our yard.

The huge metal gates, with their faded terra-cotta paint, opened wide for us to enter. The house and yard were a stark contrast to what I had seen outside the wall. The yard was a beautiful, verdant expanse with blooming tropical shrubs lining the walls. Just past the tile-roofed gazebo, young fruit trees stood in rows like troops awaiting inspection. I liked the large expanse of carport patio area under the house which offered a constant breeze. I could see this area used during hot weather. Satisfied with the grounds, I turned my attention to the house. The four-year-old coat of paint gave evidence to the lack of mercy from the tropical sun, so paint would need to be high on the list of priorities if the wooden railings of the veranda were to be protected. I climbed the stairs to the living area of the house; my critical eye, developed by years of living in older homes, searched the structure and assessed the need for repairs.

It took a moment to adjust from the bright sunlight to the dimmer light inside as I stepped through the door. The large overhang from the veranda shaded the interior from the intense rays of the sun, a blessing this close to the equator. As my eyes became accustomed to the light, I became aware of the vastness of the room before me. Including the open-walled kitchen, it must have claimed over half of the twenty-five hundred square foot floor space. There were three doors in the living/dining area; one door exited to the veranda front entry and another to the side of the veranda for the rear yard. The last door, the one nearest the kitchen, offered a twelve-foot drop to the ground. We immediately dubbed it "The Zen Door." It pleased me to see the floors were terrazzo. Our house in Florida had them and once polished, they become almost maintenance free. Every wall of every room was painted the same color: melon. The vastness of the rooms made almost any color seem too much but, in this case, the state of the walls gave the appearance that the melon had become overripe. The master bedroom was immense; it was twice the size of our living room in Hawai'i. The adjoining bath was also large but a huge garden Jacuzzi tub and the steps that led up to it consumed the floor space. The plumbing fixtures were mediocre by U.S. standards but above average by Honduran values. The small amount of furniture we had negotiated for had become quite sparse by the time we arrived. We were left with two beds, a sofa and love seat, a coffee table minus the glass top, four bar stools and a handmade Honduran table too tall to eat at and too large to place against a wall. We also found some dated electronic equipment for direct TV and pieces of a phone service we could not understand. There would be plenty to do and lots of space to do it in. These items were the seeds that would help create our new life.

The sound of Ordin's footsteps coming down the rear stairs brought me back to the present. He was up and ready to locate some coffee to start his day. Having him in the yard with Pu and me gave the morning less of a feeling of strangeness. As the sun rose to make its appearance and the strange new neighborhood noises began, Pueo was ready to have her breakfast and retreat to the mahogany closet that she claimed as her sanctuary. Oscar had managed to contact us and grabbed the last bus from San Pedro Sula to La Ceiba, arriving at the house late the evening before. He would not be ready to join us for a while. I was sure that he was awake but this was his quiet time as well. Today he and I would visit with the caretaker and create a contract; Oscar was stern about suggesting a contract when people hiring people to work. Suddenly there was a sound at the gate; it told me the caretaker was arriving and the morning had begun.

The Caretaker

This house had been under the care of the same man for the last eight years. Hired by the original owner, he stayed as an employee of the second. Now the time had come to decide whether he would stay with the third. I love to garden and enjoyed the challenge of hand clearing and planting our acre of paradise in Hawai'i, but the weariness of keeping a parcel this size had me ready to hang up my gardening gloves. I liked the idea of someone doing the heavier work, but my yard is a sacred place to me; the person who tended it needed a gentle spirit.

I knew very little about the man I would be speaking with today. He lived in the town, had poor eyesight and had requested a raise to stay. I would need to see if he merited a raise. The yard was beautiful and well tended, but I could not have the detached attitude of many people who employ property help. If this man stayed on, I knew he would become part of our family; for that reason, I wanted this interview. He introduced himself as Cesár when we arrived the previous day. His demeanor seemed quiet and unassuming but I needed time in the yard and with him to get a true feeling for his character. He had shown me around the grounds when we arrived, trying to teach me the Spanish words for oranges, grapefruit and cinnamon. He seemed polite, but I was much too fractured from the journey to make any assessment then.

Now, sitting across from him less than twenty-four hours later, I found myself impressed by his calm and gentle manner. His bearing was respectful but not subservient; he appeared to be at peace with whom he was, and willing to allow others their space. He stood five-foot-seven with the ever-present hat removed from his short, curly, black hair. His sturdy, average build and the texture of his coffee-colored skin implied a vitality that would complement a man ten years his junior. My morning walk in the yard offered insight about the caliber of attention he gave the property, and talking with him through Oscar's translations, I was now learning a bit of his history.

Cesár was born fifty years earlier in the wooden dwelling that still stands along the riverbank behind our house, and had lived most of his life in Porvenir. He and his wife had raised their three children in a small, concrete block home that was within walking distance from our house. He wanted us to know that he was not politico, he would not refer people to do work, and even though he had a personal relationship with the Creator, he did not attend church. After those simple statements, he added that he would like to stay on as caretaker, explaining that it was difficult for a man, even with full sight, to find a job after the age of fifty. It had been five years since his last raise and he also needed some time in the schedule for him to work his own acreage. He would like to have those requests considered in our agreement.

Besides caring for the property, Cesár had slept in one of the downstairs rooms of the house, protecting it whenever the owners were away. He gave it the care and attention that his grown children no longer needed. His integrity, knowledge, and love of the land showed in the vitality of the plant life that grew in this tropical enclave. The impression I had received from my morning walk was the caretaker of this land was the heart of the property. He was loyal to the property owners, known and respected throughout the village, and loved by dogs and children. What more could I ask? Oscar agreed with me that it would be a tremendous loss if this dedicated individual was to leave. His knowledge of the house would help us learn its idiosyncrasies and he could act as liaison between the community and us. We also chose to use the prefix of *don* when addressing him. It was the title of respect for a wise teacher and elder. Don Cesár would get the raise he asked for and time to work his farm. The contract we created would end his workday at two in the afternoon, but allowed for exceptions if we needed to be away. A clause in his contract requested he take Ordin canoeing on the river occasionally; don Cesár loved including that part. He was now part of the family.

la Playa—The Beach

I had not seen the beach yet and wanted to establish a daily routine of walking the shoreline, one of the daily routines I missed in Hawai'i from our life in Florida. Kenton, our buyer agent, had mentioned after his first inspection that it was a "low quality beach," meaning that it had coarse, brown sand which contained some rocks. I could live with that. It could not be any worse than some of the results of the refurbishing done to many Florida beaches, plus we were used to an island with very little beach. I was already in shorts and a tee so I grabbed my beach hat, determined to start my habit.

The distance from the house to the beach area was roughly one-and-a- half city blocks, but this was definitely not the city. When I first stepped out of the gates, I saw the evidence of recent cow traffic. In fact, a wobble-legged calf still stood in the shade of our wall as though wondering where the rest of the herd had gone. As I walked to the beach, much of my attention was on where to place my sandaled feet, picking my way past the cattle droppings and over the large round stones that formed the roadbed. My stride was moderate but I slowed my pace when I came on something of interest. Once past my neighbor's house, there were about two hundred yards of pasture and shade trees before the next home. In the distance it took to reach the beach, there were only four houses, the last one being the property of a church missionary. Each of the houses appeared nicely designed and well-kept; obviously, this was the more affluent area of Porvenir. Like a self-appointed, one-woman Garden Committee, I admired, studied and made mental notes of their gardens and landscaping, gathering possible ideas that don Cesar and I might use.

As I approached the beach, I spotted two open-air cantinas, one containing a large dance floor. The smaller of the two was near the mouth of the river within a stone's throw of the ocean. It had a thatch roof, sand floor and hammocks hanging along the riverside. The owner was buying fresh fish from one of the local anglers, which meant there would be *pescado* on the menu today. As I turned to look past the large cantina to the full panorama of the beach, my heart sank. What I saw dismayed me. How ugly! There was no way that anyone could enjoy this beach. The shock had my feet riveted while my mind sought order for my thoughts. I saw plastic bottles, tree limbs and trash of all sorts strewn up and down the beach. "Low quality beach?" "There is NO quality to this beach." was my first impression as my eyes took in the scene before me. As the shock faded away and logic overrode my travel weary nerves, I began to realize what I was seeing and my sense of calm returned. It was storm debris. I was witnessing the remnants of the hurricane surf that had swept up the coast to Cancun. With the hurricane rubble was the effect of Honduras's own winter storms. Tree limbs, huge bamboo roots and plastic waste were all over the beach. This realization helped the scene before me make more sense, but even rationalized thought could not totally override my feeling of loss. I wanted my love of the beach to compensate for all the other minor disappointments, but the sight filling my eyes only added to the list.

In a calmer state, I began to study the scene. As the shock subsided, I became aware of many children at the tree line, raking the rubbish. This appeared to be a supervised school project. Amid the raking was a man carrying a large video camera on his shoulder. He was talking with the students and filming their efforts. I later learned the camera operator was interviewing these volunteers for a local TV program. Rubble, minus the hurricane addition, is the by-product of winter storms and the result of the flooded rivers flowing to the ocean along this coast. Since there is no machinery to clean the beach, volunteers from the surrounding community and schools come to rake, clean and burn. "It will all be clear by Easter; it always is." was what I heard. "There are no limits to what man can accomplish when the desire is strong enough." was the thought running through my mind as I watched the efforts at what appeared to be an insurmountable task. It would be a wonder if they could meet their deadline.

Walls and Bars

It is a longtime habit in most well-to-do Spanish communities to have bars on the windows and a security wall around the property. Often, the exterior of the house will even look less than cared for to discourage anyone on the outside from knowing the wealth contained within the walls. To me, it seems that all this security only advertises wealth but, for hundreds of years, there have only been the rich and the poor in many South and Central American countries, so walls are protection. It is not easy to get used to, but even monasteries have walls, I guess.

The walls around our place are common concrete block. I can see by the pattern that it was first intended to be just three feet tall; possibly the builder had planned to put ornate concrete pillars above the solid wall as I have seen around other houses. Regardless of the intent, it is now eight feet of block with a coil of barbed wire across the top. If it was up to me, the wire would come down. Even though it is not uncommon to see it spiraling along the tops of walls in many homes, to me it belies the "*¡Buenos Dias!*" I prefer a sense of community and see the walls as a hindrance and the wire communicating a message of "stay out." But, like Pueo, I am new to this environment and will take each season cautiously and learn about this country before making too many big changes.

The woman who lives behind the wall next door seems to know everyone and is quite comfortable with the country lifestyle of Porvenir. She is a tall, attractive woman in her early thirties, with long, chestnut-colored hair that she keeps pulled away from her classic features in a "no-nonsense" way. She is the mother of two and manages an empire consisting of three horses, two parrots and four dogs, as well as the house staff and various migrant inhabitants of her property. Since her husband is away for months at a time with his work, she is very accomplished at delegating and multitasking. She is originally from Roatan Island, where they primarily speak English, so along with Oscar she has helped introduce us to the family across the way and the stonemason on my other side. Everyone I have met here has been friendly, offering assistance if we need it.

One evening we found ourselves visiting in the general roadway in front of our properties, a common occurrence on warm-weather evenings. The discussion eventually turned to the merits and problems of walls, when the man across the way mentioned his desire to build one around his property. I responded, through translation, with the difficulty I felt in knowing the community when hidden on one side of a wall. At that point, the man gently suggested that I get a Spanish dictionary and then use the gate. Simply stated but true; walls are like any other barriers between people—they only have the importance we give them. He had seen what I had chosen to deny; the greatest wall was my insecurity.

The Housekeeper

Have you ever lived in a household with a daily housekeeper or a cook, other than your mom? I had not since I left home. I have had help with cleaning on a once-a-week or every-two-weeks basis but I have never had an actual housekeeper or cook. During the time we were in Hawai'i, I had done so much cooking that I decided, "If I never prepare more than a peanut butter sandwich ever again, I will die happy." Once this was decided, I announced to Ordin that I had promised myself the treat of a housekeeper-cook when we got to Honduras, and from what I had heard of the wages there, it would be completely affordable.

Now the time was here to fulfill this desire, but the timing was not appropriate since our cookware and other personal belongings were still in transit. However, since Oscar would not be with us forever and I could not conduct an interview alone, we decided to do it right away. Oscar had put the word out through the village that I was looking for help, knowing that it would shortly reach the ears of any interested people. Within forty-eight hours, the pineapple wireless had done its work and an attractive, shy, young woman, her daughter and mother-in-law showed up to interview us. They wanted to know what work we offered, and then they would decide which of them was best suited for the position. We explained what we were looking for and then Oscar set a time for them to return the next day; we would then interview them. He felt it was important to take charge of the situation right away.

The women arrived at the gate within minutes of the appointed time the next evening; this was a good sign. As I mentioned earlier, Honduran time is rather casual, so to be late for this meeting would not have been the best start for either of us. Living with Hawaiian folk for years had already prepared me to expect a number of family members to show up for the interview, so when the small delegation arrived, Oscar and I gathered plastic chairs so we could all sit on the veranda. I admire the protection and support the families offer one another. The two women had decided between themselves that the younger one, Rosanna, was best suited for the work we wanted done.

She was twenty-one, with beautiful black hair that she confined at the back of her head with a clip. Her figure had the rounded contours that so many Honduran women's bodies claimed after childbirth. Rosanna, her husband and four-year-old daughter lived in a little wooden house along a small river, just behind the home of her in-laws. She loved to cook, and had learned food preparation in one of the popular local restaurants, but the twelve-to-sixteen-hour days the job often demanded allowed little time for family and it became impossible for her to remain there. Her only other work experience was in the pineapple fields when she was a teenager, helping to support her family after her father died.

There would be only one month to teach her the routines of our household before I would need to leave her and meet my group in Mexico for our retreat. Ordin and I did not have many appliances but it would take some time to introduce her to a microwave and an automatic washing machine. She, like most of the local women, did her laundry in a washtub that sat in the yard and found little need for a microwave oven in her lifestyle. Many of the women in the country use outdoor ovens. We decided to leave the menu up to her for the first month so we could sample local foods and learn her preferences. I had already settled, through Oscar, that we would not want to eat hot spicy food, and that we preferred not to eat the more unusual body parts of animals. I had eaten my token amount of raw fish and octopus while in Hawai'i and was not sure how Honduran tastes ran. I wanted to approach that subject right away since the economy of the country inclined me to believe that they wasted nothing. Everyone on the veranda shook with laughter as the gringo lady offered to pass on to them any tongue or stomach that might offer to her. They explained that hot spicy food was not the custom here and most of the meat was *pollo* (chicken) and seafood.

There was only one last concern I had not addressed and that was our privacy. If I took on a household domestic, what would become of our personal space? For years our daily lives had revolved around only the three of us. Living in the jungles of Hawai'i, we seldom had casual drop-ins; people came for a reason, which had an allotted time, then they would leave. We occasionally had parties when people would stay much longer, but even then, it was one day. Now I was about to commit to a daily routine with an extra person IN THE HOUSE.

One of the forms of entertainment Ordin and I have is watching a BBC movie in the evening. Through this form of entertainment, I also get a lot of insight into the lives of British gentry. Invariably, their homes have some amount of domestic help and I have often wondered how they keep their privacy while maintaining a household staff. I was well past needing to be sold on the idea of being free from dealing with everyday necessities; it would be wonderful to have my time free for writing, studies and my workshops. The house was large enough to require some help, but I wondered how large it needed to be to not trip over the help. The best solution seemed to be having her come within Don Cesar's hours: an hour after he arrives, which would give Ordin, Pu and me about three hours to spend quiet time outside and get our breakfast out of the way. Rosanna would then come in to clean the house, do laundry and prepare our noon meal. She would have lunch with us before cleaning up the kitchen; that would allow her to leave at one o'clock, one hour before Cesar went home. She would have the afternoon free to care for her personal demands and our home would be ours, alone, again. Our evening meal does not require help since our habit is to have a light snack. This routine seemed to complement her family's needs as well as ours, and she was willing to stay extra time if we had a special occasion. We agreed and the contract written.

Wildlife

Ordin and I have always enjoyed bird and animal watching in each of the areas we have lived. We especially enjoy sharing our morning coffee time with the wildlife foraging for their own breakfast. The array of color offered by the various butterflies throughout the yard is a thrill to see, and because of the house's close proximity to the river we are able to watch the habits of a number of beautiful bird species. Condors and herons pass over the yard on their way to the marsh fields and huge trees that lean across the river; wild parrots make a twice-daily appearance when traveling to their feeding spots. An unusually brilliant yellow and white bird with bold, black markings has added to our study. It was a thrill to again see a robin, even though it was a new variety to us, as well as the red crown of flickers. I had not realized that their absence left such a void during our Hawai'i years. The aerial acrobatics of the hummingbirds are a source of entertainment for us and a fascination for Pueo as they visit our hibiscus each morning and evening. The often hover to scold Pueo or us if we allow her to violate their space. We found many birds that are new to us and we are astounded to find that all the birds here share the habit of being more aggressive than our Hawai'i or Florida birds; even the usually docile doves stand their ground.

Meanwhile, my neighbor's parrots offered daily amusement. Their home was a huge cage that sat on the lawn next to the wall that divided our yards. The parrots' voices responding to the yard activity, created a scenario in my mind of two old crones cast under a magical spell, condemned to feathered bodies until they are able to redeem themselves. Having the parrots next door became a plus by increasing my new vocabulary. They greeted everyone with *"¡Hóla, Hóla!"* to try to entice susceptible subjects to their cage and then laugh outrageously as though they have played a nasty trick. As the security dogs were released for the evening, the birds' exaggerated, hysterical warnings of *"¡Perro, perro, perro!"* have etched the Spanish word for dog permanently into my nervous system. This feathered duo also conversed with each other in a Roatan dialect so rapid that their owner had yet to understand all they were saying. Their repertoire included the names of her children, the sound of a tricycle bell, a car alarm, a ringing cell phone and wolf whistles which rewarded me as I walked out on my veranda each morning.

Birds are just part of the aerial nature in our neighborhood. It surprised me to see the number of bats that swooped through the evening sky, retarding the mosquito population. Admiring their airborne exhibitions in the early morning and evening made me wonder where they all live; the population would suggest a possible cave nearby. Nevertheless, I was glad to have their voracious appetites cleaning the airways over the yard, even if their numbers were vaguely overwhelming.

One morning, as Pueo and I took our early morning walk around the yard, I heard something hit the metal roof of our home. Strange; but then it happened again, and again. As I walked around the side of the house to investigate, I saw bats at the eaves! They were getting into our attic space! "Stop them." was my only thought! By this time, Ordin was coming down with his morning coffee, and together, we stared in disbelief. These pesky varmints had found a loose edge where the new metal roof was improperly attached along the rim. While the house had sat, more often than not unoccupied for two years, these winged mammals had taken up residency. A neighbor brought an extension ladder and a piece of molding strip, trying to seal the edge of the roof, but once bats have taken up residency, their tiny minds are hard to change. If there was another weak place in the roof, they would find it.

A few nights later, I awakened to the sound of scratching on the walls. It is Pueo's habit to sometimes do that to get our attention, so this is what I expected to find as I sat up to get out of bed. I tried to locate her in the darkness of our room but she was not there, and neither was the noise. The scratching noise echoed off the concrete walls and through the house, still devoid of furniture. Slowly, I followed the sound to what I felt was its source and found Pueo staring at the ceiling. Something was definitely up there, dancing around with enough enthusiasm that a ceiling tile was coming loose. I propped a mop from windowsill to ceiling and told Pu to come back to bed. We would need to wait until morning. Ewww, bats! This was going to take a team effort. Our priority list was growing.

Tomorrow morning we would ask Oscar to help us find an exterminator, and carpenters that could seal off every access. Thank goodness he had come. I am not sure what we would have done without his friendly manner and fluent Spanish. He introduced us to the neighbors and helped interview don Cesár and the new housekeeper-cook who would soon begin. He rode to town with Ordin each day to expedite services, wrote contracts and helped us make connections. Tomorrow afternoon he would be leaving. Part of me was ready for the quieter pace that would come when his robust personality returned to the U.S., yet a greater part of me worried about being on our own. Nevertheless, it had to happen.

We would never learn all we needed to know while protected by this guardian spirit. Sometimes at night, when I would lie down to sleep, a subtle feeling of depression would cover me; this new life was all so overwhelming. There was too much to learn and assimilate too fast. I could certainly empathize with Pu. Would we ever get past this? The quiet part of my mind told me that a day would come when I would look back to this time and see a lighter side. I hoped so.

Week Two

Hardware Shopping

This week started out with projects. There is always so much to do when you buy an older home...plus my Ordin loves a project; he can never be still. The water pump in the laundry room had been whining as though it had worn blades and needed to be replaced. Ordin had already contracted with a young man and his crew to start repairing and securing the roofline and tile the veranda. They would not start until next week and he could not wait another day to quiet down that pump. My husband is a multi-talented guy with experience in multiple fields, many involving forms of construction, so I do not get too concerned when he takes on something new. Before I had realized his expertise however, he could set my teeth on edge using a skill saw or a drill around my favorite pieces of furniture, but now he has proven himself to have a keen eye and a master's touch when he takes on a project.

So, I was not too concerned when he said he could not wait any longer for someone else to repair that pump. Still, navigating through most hardware stores in Honduras can be a new experience for Americans. In the U.S., it is a simple matter of deciding what you want and wandering the isles until you find it. Sometimes, if you are lucky, a clerk can help you locate what you are searching for and possibly offer guidance when multiple selections require a decision. At the hardware store Ordin went to in La Ceiba, a clerk takes care of everything for you. You simply tell him what you want or give him a list. He will delegate plumbing parts to a person in that department, painting items to someone from that department, and so on. Then, when it is time to pay for your selections, all of these people bring their items to the pickup counter where each item is tested and tallied. It is at this point that you and your money part ways and you collect your goods.

It seems like a wonderful system. It controls thefts and returns, as well as serves customers faster, therefore making happy patrons... unless there is a language barrier. Usually, my husband seeks out an

English-speaking salesclerk he has worked with before, but she is not always available. For the most part, Ordin has started having the bilingual construction boss he hired make a list for him in Spanish to present to the clerks; however, what should have been a cunning plan has fallen short of success. On four separate occasions, O has asked to have 40-watt lightbulbs included on his shopping list. When he enters the hardware store, an efficient clerk smiles, takes the list and issues orders to waiting department clerks. When all the articles are gathered and brought to the original clerk, he and an associate go over the list together, checking off each item ordered. "*Si, si, si si* ...."—everything is in order. The cashier totals the bill, and with a friendly smile, requests the amount due. This would all seem in perfect harmony if he ever got home with any lightbulbs. To add to his frustration, the inability to read Spanish keeps him from knowing if lightbulbs were even placed on the original list. After one of these seemingly efficient whirlwind frenzies, he has become so disoriented that, when he reaches the checkout point, he cannot even recall what was originally on his list. It is only after returning to the calmer setting of home that he begins to realize that something is amiss; of course, by that time, he usually cannot find his first shopping list. For this reason, I was a little apprehensive about his taking on the new pump installation on his own; what if he needed additional parts?

As it was, the project went fairly smooth. It began with finding that he had bought the wrong size fittings, but he managed to compensate well enough with parts on hand so that water was available in the house again. Not needing to be on call, I had busied myself in the kitchen practicing Spanish with a friend. After a bit, I became vaguely aware of a curious noise coming from the front of the house but assumed it was Ordin's work in the laundry room underneath. After a few minutes more, the noise had grown to be quite a distraction...enough that I felt it warranted investigation. Following the sound, I walked down the hall and then turned the corner to enter the master bedroom. I stopped. My brain could not absorb what my eyes were seeing. The room was filling with water. All command of my budding Spanish vanished as the only words I could manage to yell were, "WATER! SHUT IT OFF! SHUT OFF THE WATER!"

The hot waterline to the master bathroom sink had broken loose under the greater pressure of the new pump and the entire west floor of the room was underwater. Since our personal items had not yet arrived, my friend and I were limited to only two towels and a couple of old, threadbare mops to soak, sop and mop up gallons of water. It took almost an hour for us to dry the floor. My sense of humor and state of calm were as tightly wrung as the old mops had been, but I do remember hearing once that memorization is always easier when associated with an emotion. I know I will not forget that *agua* means water.

A Car

Our choice to live in the country meant that we had to either learn the bus schedule or get a car. Ordin opted for the car. In fact, he traveled into La Ceiba with the van drivers the afternoon we arrived at the house and immediately rented a car. Ordin is a very confident driver; you might even say he has nerves of steel, which is a definite asset in Honduran traffic. As I mentioned earlier, driving through this country is a mastered art of "right-of-way by intimidation." All the drivers I have seen seem friendly and are more than willing to let you know when you have chosen the wrong direction on any of the one-way streets, but driving through the city takes on the intensity of a nine-year-old boy playing Nintendo. We also learned that most people do not insure their cars; if some choose to, it is for only repair or replacement, so when we discussed buying a car we chose to purchase something used.

The car rental agency told us that they sell their over-mileage cars along the road outside town. That was one option. We could also be on the lookout for cars marked with *se vende*, "for sale," on the windows. Ordin had rented our car for only a two-week period and even though we could pay to extend the lease, it seemed that we should start making car shopping a priority. We certainly ran to town enough to have looked for a car, but the used car lots that are so plentiful in the U.S. are much less available here. No matter how much time we allowed for errands, it never seemed to be enough. In Hawai'i, folks often saved money by buying cars on the mainland and shipping them to the islands; that might be a consideration here. We could shop for a car in Texas or Florida and pay to have it brought in, but the shipping cost added to the customs fees, compounded by any language difficulty, made us hesitate.

As the sand drained from our "rental" hourglass and my mind was consumed with this problem, we found ourselves needing to make a trip to Ceiba again, this time because friends needed to shop for groceries. Ordin was lucky enough to find parking under a huge tree, so he and I opted to sit in the car to wait. As we sat talking, I happened to notice a cute, little, metallic green Kia Sport in the parking lot with *se vende* written on the window. I was particularly drawn to the size of the vehicle since the last auto we had owned was a huge, dual-cabin, full-size, four-by-four pickup. It turned like a tank and was intimidating to parallel park. If I were ever going to drive on the busy streets of La Ceiba, I would need something that could slip into small spaces easily. This little sparkler looked like it could meet the four-wheel drive requirements of my husband, yet yielded itself to my level of confidence. We had already looked into the Kia line in Hawai'i when a dealership first opened, so we were familiar with the brand. It seemed to me that synchronicity was at work here and that we needed to trust Honduras to meet our needs, so I prodded Ordin, encouraging him to walk over and take a closer look at the little car. As he walked around the car, running his eyes over the exterior of the body, the owner showed up to open the doors. The owner spoke no English and Ordin was still limited in his degree of Spanish, but data was recorded while some stumbling conversation and phone numbers were exchanged. All we needed now was to find another English-speaking amigo.

It took a few days to create the arena that would allow us to make a final decision. We could not get a translator, a car owner and a firm knowledge of the law together all at one time. In addition, the car was never in one place. So each time we wanted to see the owner or the car we had to find a translator and have them call the owner. Then wait until he drove to our location from wherever it was the car was parked at that moment. I was beginning to feel that my senses had failed me; this transaction was requiring more effort than I felt it should take. Old stories of corruption south of the border began to haunt me and my brain began to question the legality of the sale. We decided to go see our friend Kent; he would be able to answer our questions.

It was the perfect moment to catch him in his office. He looked up from his stack of papers, smiling at being rescued from the task at hand. Our concern must have shown on our faces as he suggested we sit down. We presented our problem to him and explained our uneasiness. What we learned from him was that this scenario was not unusual; in Honduras, not all business is done behind a desk. The process that was feeling so clumsy to us was not atypical at all for Honduran negotiations. On further investigation, we found the owner of the car was actually a used car dealer. The reason the car had been so difficult to locate when we wanted to see it was because he kept his overhead down by parking or driving the cars around town for visibility. That information removed a major concern, so now, with most of our questions answered and the negotiations finished, it was time for the final decision. We calculated Lempira to Dollars and headed to the ATM machine to use our International card.

The little Kia was ours! I do not know if our excitement was for finally buying a car or for having met the challenge of the transaction. The thrill was even sweeter when we learned the lawyer's fees for the title switch and purchase of tags had been part of the selling price. Now we would get to take it out on the highway, through the bus traffic and potholes, to see how well it would fare on the journey to El Porvenir. Trepidation turned into assurance and then spread into pleasure, as under Ordin's fearless hands, our little gem maneuvered past every obstacle and danced around each hazard. We had trusted our intuition and let our instincts guide us, the outcome of which confirmed again that we must be in the right place. Our pleasure with the car has continued to grow as we drive it. With a couple of minor repairs and the maintenance needed owing to the roads of Porvenir, we can view this acquisition as another triumph placed on the success side of our balance scale.

The First Shipment Arrives

I knew this would happen. No matter how much logic I employed with my selection of items to ship, when they arrived it would be a very different person receiving the shipment on this end. That is exactly how it felt. Have you ever received a gift for your home from someone you barely know? Most often you may find yourself wondering, "Whatever possessed them to pick THAT?" Well, the first shipment of boxes has arrived and this is precisely what I am thinking. The person who sent those boxes did not know what my life was going to be like here.

These are the boxes I had sent six weeks earlier. Of course, they would not hold my most essential items since I had wanted to use those until the last, right? One of my Hawai'i neighbors had offered to loan us some pots and pans or whatever else we might need, allowing us to ship our most necessary items sooner, but I just was not ready to do that. Now I kill time, making due on this end while I wait for our cookware, silverware, cutlery, and business computer disks. The ideal solution would have been to rent a place in Honduras for a month or so before we ever moved here to find what we would consider a necessity here. We would have gotten more feel for the kinds of items that are accessible and what was going to be indispensable. Ordin had planned to scout the stores for me, but between his lost wallet and his untrained eye for household needs, I never learned how precious were the cutting boards, kitchen strainers, silverware trays, and all the tools we gave away. I did not pack any of these; they are available everywhere, correct? Wrong. Now, as I await the basic items of Western life, I mentally entertain myself with thoughts of traveling to the U.S. and buying out some discount store so I can open my own business here, offering those "quality" plastic items.

At least this shipment supplied me with plenty of towels and some drinking glasses. I had already bought dishes here rather than take the chance of shipping. This was one of my wiser decisions, since in unpacking my boxes, I have come to the realization there is no sense in trying to transport anything glass or ceramic, including framed pictures with glass. No matter how well I packed any form of breakable, it was not able to survive being in the bottom box under a pile of fifteen. My little hand-etched drinking glasses, a gift from one of my clients, survived only because they came packed in their own styrofoam box within the larger box. I have noticed the words *Fragil* and "fragile" look almost the same, but in my using the "e", it must have distorted the meaning for the freight forwarders. The second shipment will come in plastic bins, which was an excellent idea, only the canvas tarp and cookware they contain hardly need the extra protection. I have one more month to wait until that second shipment arrives with all my crucial items. Meanwhile, I can while away the hours reading my books, dusting my rice paper art, fluffing my handmade throw pillows, or playing my ukulele.

Week Three

The Birthday Card

Tuesday, or *martes*, is don Cesár's birthday. Honduran laborers are entitled to a number of paid holidays but birthdays are not one of them. Ordin and I wanted to do something to recognize the occasion but did not feel we knew him well enough to buy a gift. We had discussed it with Oscar; he discouraged giving money. I began placing "a Spanish birthday card" on every errand list the guys took to town long before Oscar returned to the States. However, with all the other demands on everyone's time, this request had slipped from the priority list. Now the birthday was quickly approaching, and if we were going to do this, we needed to find a card soon. After hours of thought and discussion, we finally settled on giving don Cesár the day off from work but I wanted to make sure this was communicated clearly.

Just the week before, Ordin and I decided we should try walking the beach each morning before the heat and business of the day started. I had not been back since my first venture out and really wanted to get a routine set up. We felt we should wait until don Cesár arrived so we could tell him that we would be down to the beach for a while in case he needed us. As he let himself through the gate that morning, we met him in our shorts and suits at the base of the stairs. After an exchange of morning greetings, we practiced our dictionary-perfect Spanish by stating, "*caminar la playa*"; "Walk the beach" was the book translation. Of course we gestured back and forth to each other, saying our names. All three of us were smiling as Ordin and I walked out of the gate. We were pleased to have the morning to ourselves but equally pleased that we were getting such a smooth grip on this new language; it was a real milestone. We were doubly pleased with don Cesár's smile as a reward for our efforts. Our return home an hour later turned our self-satisfaction into dismay as we found a very disappointed Cesár, in shorts and tank top, trying to understand what had happened to our invitation to walk to the beach. Therefore, you can see why I was a bit concerned with how to give him a day off without communicating, "Happy Birthday, you don't have a job anymore."

Ordin and I made a trip to La Ceiba specifically to hunt for the birthday card. I have yet to find anything in the town that would be the equivalent of a card store or even a stationery store. I did remember the two good department stores I had seen offered a gift wrapping service and reasoned that part of gifts were cards. Sure enough, we found a small selection of cards at the Carrion store. Wisely, I had thought to bring along our Spanish dictionary. I made sure Ordin put it into the car as I opened the gate for us to leave the house. As we stood facing the meager selection of cards, all of which were in Spanish, each of us looked at the other, expecting the dictionary; we were on the second floor, middle of the mall...it was still in the car.

The feeling of being lost at sea, which had become so familiar of late, washed over me once more. We were on our own again. Rather than give up or do something really wise like return to the car, we started using a process of elimination. We passed over the juvenile cartoons and any cards with *Mamma, Papa* or *Señorita*, until we found one with *Amigo*. The picture was beautiful and looked so much like the view of the other side of the river where don Cesár had taken Ordin canoeing, but there were an awful lot of words besides *Feliz Cumpleaños, Amigo*. We carried it to the cashier and asked if it would be a fitting card for a man who had recently become our friend. Her smile was apologetic as she said the words we had learned to expect: "*No Inglis.*" Since "*Amigo*" means friend, and in today's world friend could mean anything. We felt a sense of urgency to find someone who would confirm that this was a suitable card; one that was lacking offense, for us to give this gentle man. Without accosting all the shoppers, we asked for help from anyone who would make eye contact. An American serviceman seemed happy to connect with others from home but his command of Spanish was no greater than our own. Our looks of distress and acts of desperation finally drew the attention of a distinguished looking middle-aged man. I had noticed him earlier; he was aware of our plight but had not wanted to get involved with our plea for help. Thankful for his show of mercy, we did not bother to explain that it was for our caretaker but told him it was for a new friend who had been helping us. He did not offer to translate but, after carefully reading over the contents, stated the words were heartfelt; he judged it suitable for the relationship.

We still needed to find the correct way to tell don Cesár that he had the day off. Having exhausted all my contacts, I finally sat down with the English-Spanish dictionary to compose a letter. This was becoming a way of communication for Cesár and I. I would write out a message in Spanish with the English words over the top. He would then read to me what I had written in his language and then in mine. My words always sounded so beautiful when he spoke them and this technique seemed to be helping both of us learn; however, this time it would not be a simple message of, "It is time to mow the lawn." This would be a message of appreciation. Spanish is a beautiful language and I dream of the day I become fluent enough to express my feelings. Meanwhile, the dictionary helps with my basic messages. Pen in hand, I wrote in English the words I wanted him to read but, as I hunted for their Spanish translations, the feelings I wanted to convey became lost in the complexities of the language.

I finally settled for:

Don Cesár, Martes es tu cumpleanos.

Nosotros querer ti empezar hacer el dia libre en trabajo de sequir tu Corazon.

Feliz Cumpleanos.

Hasta el Miercoles

Ordin and Malana

To the best of our knowledge, this translated to:

Don Cesar, Tuesday is your birthday.

We want you to have the day free from work to follow your heart.

Happy Birthday.

Good-bye until Wednesday.

Ordin and Malana

The Repairs Begin

Cesár showed up for work on Wednesday. We were able to add one more small success to our balance scale and were ready to tackle another challenge: the carpenters. Our small and friendly construction crew showed up the following Monday morning to begin the repairs and improvements we had contracted. There was a construction boss and two carpenters, all related to one another. We were given an estimated time of two weeks to complete our projects, and by the end of just a few days, the crew began to feel like part of our family, often similar to having all of our kids back home. When the concept of "*siesta* time" evaporated under the influence of western business, many outdoor workers tried to follow a schedule that started in the early hours and ended about two in the afternoon. Our guys had every intention of adhering to that schedule too, but their earnest desire to be working by seven-thirty each morning settled into "Honduras time", which could be one to three hours later. Since only the crew boss had a vehicle, the carpenters were at the mercy of whatever errands their boss needed to complete each morning before arriving at the job site. Later, when the boss's truck went into the garage for repairs, these workers arrived at the job on bicycles, their meager tools toted in backpacks. It was astonishing to see these young men climbing our metal roof in the hottest part of the day, taking all the tropical sun wanted to give, without ever losing their sense of humor. Day by day, I watched them in wonder, with a growing awareness of the Honduran people.

Many of the carpenters here do not own a lot of their own tools. The average worker earns about one hundred Lempiras a day and a skilled carpenter can make forty Lempiras an hour—about two dollars U.S. Their meager wages do not allow them the excess money to invest in tools if they have families to feed, which most of them do. A hammer could cost a day's wages; an electric saw, a week's pay. Even if they ride bikes to the job, as our guys do, anything more than a hammer and saw could be cost prohibitive. In our case, it became our responsibility to supply tools. The carpenters showed up with hammers plus a well-worn electric drill, along with a desire to work, happy dispositions, and a competent level of skill. They also cleaned up their own work mess at the end of their day.

If you are a person who lives by level, square, and plumb, Honduras might have you grinding your teeth by the end of the first week. All the building here gets accomplished and done fairly competently, but the ability must be in their blood. Most of the construction is concrete because of the termites, but I never see the builders using elaborate guides, levels or lasers common in U.S.-style construction. Honduran builders also do not waste time forming openings for electrical and plumbing lines. Those are amenities that can always be added later since it makes more sense to them to let the plumber chip away at the finished concrete wall, and the same for the electrician. The job gets finished but not with the finesse that Americans consider routine. A friend here once told me that Hondurans take care of immediate problems and do not bother to project into what tomorrow might bring. Maybe that is why they are so content; after all, "Don't worry...be happy." is a Caribbean phrase.

Ordin is a recovering German cabinetmaker. This does not require him to attend meetings, but it is important that he practice controlled breathing when he looks at poor quality wood molding or handrails. His German father was a master cabinet artisan and Ordin grew up working at his side. The DNA, compounded with years of practice, has created an amazing ability to turn wood into art. The same ingredients have created intolerance for less-than-perfect work. On numerous social outings, he has drawn me aside to take me into his confidence about some viewed structural defect. His "Can you believe ...." is generally followed by my "Just take a breath."

This possibly gives some insight to the plight of our *carpinteros*. They did not speak English but their crew boss was bilingual. Ordin would tell the boss what he wanted done; the boss would relay it to the carpenters. Then Ordin and the boss would travel into town together to buy materials needed for the project. When they returned from town, invariably the instructions had not been performed to Ordin's directions. This could be due to either the crew boss not understanding or not communicating, or the carpenters not understanding the boss, the instructions, or the plan. Either way, the work would often need to be done again. Each time, Ordin would do his best to explain what had to be accomplished and how he wanted it done; the boss would say "*Si,si.*" and pass on the instructions. Ordin's understanding of Spanish is superior to mine, but I have witnessed him listening intently to a neighborhood person and repeatedly responding with "*Si,si.*" when I knew he did not *see* what the person was saying at all. Rather than frustrate the speaker, O confessed, he would rather just go along, hoping that eventually it would make sense to him. I sometimes wonder if our crew boss did not follow the same technique.

Marzo—March

Since the *Carpinteros*

For days on end, I have had carpenters crawling and banging on my roof and hanging outside my windows. There has been no sign of bats since the first day of hammering on the metal roof, and little sign of Pueo. She stays in the closet the entire day, in a mild state of shock; her system still not recovered from travel, and now construction! It seemed the situation might get even worse once the crew boss left for Roatan Island, since the carpenters would need to ride the ten miles to work by bicycle. That meant they would also begin staying later; no longer would there be an afternoon quiet time to recover from the busy noise of construction. With the boss gone, Ordin's frustrations with learning Spanish by immersion became intensified by having to practice Central American-style home inspection by immersion, since he was now the supervisor of the crew. Yet, as with most of life's challenges, they become an opportunity to grow, and Ordin's catapult into the arena as a crew boss became exactly that.

He did not have the time or patience to spend time plowing through the bilingual dictionary but found that pictures have no language barrier and worked best to explain his ideas. The work experience of the men allowed them to grasp quickly many of these new ideas, but if Ordin did not review them with the crew the following day, they would return to what they knew. There were even times when they did not follow plans because they felt another way would be prettier. Ordin learned to stay with them, almost work with them, sharing skills. Out of that time, a mutual respect for each other's knowledge arose and his Spanish improved; another success was added to our scale.

The original estimate we were given for the work had our projects taking about two weeks to complete and costing a certain amount of Lempiras, not including materials. With all of Ordin's corrections and the later supervision, it took six weeks to complete most of the work and completely drained our budget. The crew has gone on to other job sites and the house is now our own again. As I sit on the veranda enjoying the tranquility of a late spring shower, I see the porch roof still has a small leak and a couple of tiles on the steps have cracked. All in all though the education was worth it, and we will get around to fixing those—*mañana*.

Rosanna

This is Rosanna's first week. I have two weeks to train her before I surrender my home to her care and leave for my retreat in Mexico. I remember my anxiety about the constant extra person but it really is not much different from having one of the kids home again—but one who helps out and picks up after herself. It is a challenge to stay aware of where I am now living as I find Rosanna unable to adjust to the washing machine or microwave. These are all as foreign to her as Honduras is to me. Her laundry at home is washed by hand in a pan outdoors and hung across a fence or shrub. It is amazing to see how white and stain-free the clothing of Honduras folks is after seeing it lay out over boulders and shrubs to dry in the sun. Dishwashing in the country is another interesting study. Plates and such are washed in pans on a shelf that extends out the kitchen window, with any overflow of water available for passing poultry. At Rosanna's home she may cook on a propane gas stove, which could be under a shelter outdoors, or by using an outdoor oven. Even though she has worked in a local restaurant, it does not necessarily mean that she has the advantage of the conveniences we consider essential. Nonetheless, she is efficient, cheerful, and eager to learn.

She does have one point of resistance: the eagerness to learn does not extend to English. Rosanna knows no English and I of course, know *un diminuto Español*—only a tiny bit of Spanish. I devised a clever plan to help each of us learn our new languages; it was to write the English and Spanish words for different household items on sticky notes that are attached to each of the mentioned items. Of course, I could not share this brilliant plan with Rosanna since she did not understand me. I truly believe it would have been a great idea if the names of these normal kitchen and household items could have been found in my bilingual dictionary. I do not believe the one I have is designed for resident use, only tourist information.

Excellent Plan Number Two was to leave my little dictionary on the kitchen counter and show her how we could use it to look up words to simplify communication. Rosanna was more than willing to help me pronounce the Spanish words I wanted to use, but she was NOT EVEN going to attempt to try the English words. She seemed quite satisfied with her gesturing and my struggling. She probably felt she had enough to learn with microwaves, washing machines, and our lifestyle habits. So imagine my surprise and pleasure when she came to my little office space on her third day at work with the small dictionary. It was a breakthrough. I was elated! I watched over her shoulder as she carefully searched through the list of words, following her finger until she found the one she was searching for—*cumpleaños*: BIRTHDAY. Her motivation finally to pick up the dictionary was to announce that this was her birthday. I am sure it took me a moment to process through the feelings from great excitement to mild disappointment, balancing finally at satisfaction. She surrendered the dictionary to me so I could turn to the English side and quickly look up "congratulations": *felicitar a alguien* ! The salutation seemed as much for looking up the word as for the importance of the day. We celebrated the event by having lunch early and my doing the lunch clean-up while she went home early.

My momentary triumph was exactly that as, the next day, Rosanna returned to the pantomimes that had been serving her purpose earlier. Rosanna is the only other person I regularly try to communicate with, and she has decided that charades are easier than language struggles. She efficiently goes about her business, needing little guidance from me, but when she announces lunch she will say, "Malana," then point at her mouth and then over her shoulder to the dining area. This is the scenario when she asks me about anything. I really am getting quite good at this, but pantomime is not meant to be the desired result. I had tried to communicate, through a translator, that if she ever learns English she can get higher pay, but I do not believe that she sees that reality as part of her future. She is sweet natured and pleasant, but I think she has a stubborn streak that could match any of the Scotsmen in my family background.

My feelings of exasperation would come and go like the waves rolling onto the beach a block away. "Couldn't she understand I was trying to help her?" I thought. Then, as I recognized the words going through my mind, I was stunned by the truth of the situation. I was trying to help her, which meant she had a problem, which meant there was something wrong with her. How many times had I felt a sense of rejection when someone would correct me...helping me be better when I had not asked for help. I had only expected acceptance. Rosanna had applied for work, not a makeover, and I never included learning English as part of the job description. So, here I was, trying to get her to my comfort level instead of making the effort to rise to hers.

This was her country; I was the guest. This realization came with the understanding that I needed to accept her for whom she is. I stopped expecting her to learn my language and started putting more focus on me learning hers, doing no more than asking her assistance in pronouncing the Spanish words that I was practicing. Over a period of weeks, a change began to take place and she began asking me how to say the names of certain objects...in English. For whatever reason, Rosanna decided she needed to acquire this ability and had begun to study English on her own. This kind of change is the only healthy way any transformation can take place—with a desire from within. I did not come to Honduras to change anyone, except possibly myself. I wanted to learn about the people the way they are. But, if I am happy with whom I am and the way I live, who knows...someone may want to adopt some of my lifestyle, too.

Internet

Ordin has been under pressure, partially from me, to get us connected to the internet. It three weeks had gone by since any contact from family or friends, plus my retreat to Mexico was fast approaching and the attendees should have last-minute coaching. Another source of pressure comes from people who might be interested in having Ordin perform home inspections here. We would have been connected in a flash if it had been a simple process, but we are too far out of town for internet cable and we do not even have a phone line. The previous owners left behind masses and miles of cords from outdated, direct TV, and dish connections that are a complete puzzle to us. With the language barrier, we have found the people who understand our systems do not understand us; so they do not know what we want them to do.

Our neighbor's friend has a part-time, internet-related business and he told us about a new system connected through a cell phone and recommended we look into it. This sounded perfect, but I had learned that my perception of perfection was not always attainable in Honduras. When I had wanted a phone line, Ordin wanted cell phones. I, personally, did not care what phones we got as long as I was able to make a call when I wanted to. Out-of-country calls are expensive so I understood that they would need to be limited to necessities, but I did want to have that ability. Well, we got cell phones...they cannot call out of the country, hence the pressure for internet.

After Ordin learned of this latest development in modern technology, he picked up his bilingual amigo and headed to Ceiba to buy yet another cell phone, the brand that was necessary to do the internet thing. One frustrated attempt to connect after another led him back to town, again picking up the amigo to return to the cell phone store. By the end of the next day we had connection! I emailed my children, our business associates, and responded to waiting e-mail; I was in cyber heaven. That lasted for two days and then—no service again. My Captain Internet responded to my distress call by pitting his wits and savvy against this cell system from hell all weekend long, only to find ourselves discouraged and frustrated on Monday morning as we loaded the little system into the car and headed once again to Ceiba.

This time we got one of the ladies from Kent's office to go with us to the cell phone store. The gals that work for Kent are skilled at handling clients with kid gloves, ramrodding contractors, and keeping their boss on track. I was sure one of them could cut through all the puzzling internet jargon and obtain the answers needed. Sure enough, once language was not an issue and the right questions were asked, we found that this new aspect of the phone system was free. There was only a charge for the minutes to make phone calls but none for the internet connection. Therefore, EVERYONE was online. Not only were lots of folks using free internet service, but I am sure many them were guaranteeing internet availability by keeping the service online. Trying to change that would be as futile as trying to halt a hurricane with a stop sign. I was confident that now that we had discovered what the problem was, my Captain Internet could devise a clever plan to overcome the situation, and that is exactly what he did. The simple solution was to go online when Pueo woke us at four in the morning; no one in their right mind was going to be sitting at the computer at that time of the day...only loco gringos, so of course there would be much less competition for space.

The Neighbors

The more I venture out, the more intrigued I become with my Honduran neighbors. Our lives seem so different. "Will we ever fit in?" I wonder. The neighbors closest to us are interested in meeting us and finding out who we are; those who are a block or two away are more detached, unsure of why we are here until we smile and say *"¡Buenos!"* to them. That is the icebreaker.

The people of El Porvenir always respond to our greetings in a friendly manner. It is only natural that they would expect the first effort to be made by us; after all, we gringos are the oddity here. Ordin and I have found that we are not the only folks from the U.S. living in Porvenir, but we are still a rarity. One day I walked the half mile through town to shop at the mini-super center. It pleasantly surprised many my neighbors, including our staff. The occasion was Ordin's birthday and I was missing the tomatoes and pasta needed to prepare one of his favorite meals. As I walked the dusty road past the free-roaming dogs and horses, I found myself enjoying the short outing that brought me to the open doorway of the store. I carefully stepped past the young pig that slept in the morning sun near the entry and worked my way alongside the chickens that had raced me to the door. Once inside the doorway, as my eyes became used to the dim interior, I became aware of several early patrons. Edging my way past the other shoppers, I could see their sideways smiles, even though they acted like the sight of my shopping there was an average occurrence. I wandered up and down the three isles and found the selection of pasta, then ambled over to the fresh produce. A clever young man of about nine helped me select and weigh my tomatoes, then he led me to the checkout. I stood for a while, trying to distinguish the business from the social clientele, until finally the group parted, offering me access to the cashier. Spanish numbers still confound me, with Hondureños speaking the most rapidly of all Central Americans. So when my purchases were tallied and the amount trilled to me, I am sure my struggles to understand became a source of entertainment and conversation once I had left.

As I struggle to make social pleasantries, the people in the area reward me with smiles and offer corrections. It is a blessing to have the young mom next door to be so openhearted and fluent in English. I feel that I am just one more of the grateful who follow in the wake of her knowledge and expertise. She has been my source for answers on utility bills and nursery plants, among thousands of other things. She always tries to introduce me to some of my other neighbors if we run across them while she and I are out, but often the introduction gets lost in the information around it so I just smile and say "*¡Hóla!*" It seems to be appropriate for most occasions.

One neighbor I met across the way has about a dozen milk cows. He does not keep them on his house property, but a well-worn path running alongside his dwelling testifies to the daily milking ritual. Every morning he releases his cows from one of the grassy lots in the village to walk to the milking area behind his home. Once finished, he herds them down the road, past the *cantinas* on the beach, to a point where the river runs into the ocean. There he drives them across the river to pasture on the other side. In the early evening, the cows swim the river again, returning to home pasture. Our cat, Pueo, has assumed the responsibility of supervisor, intently watching the ankles of our "Ladies of Lactose" as they pass our gate each morning and evening. As a gesture of friendliness, this neighbor knocked on the gate one morning with a gift of fresh, whole milk. Mmm, I had forgotten how wonderful real milk tastes. Now this man is my dairyman and every Monday I can be found en route along the trail that "Our Ladies" have trod for years to collect two liters of fresh, whole milk for twenty Lempiras—about one U.S. dollar.

The neighbors to the south side of me are an enclave. A young man introduced himself to Oscar and me the day after we arrived. He was adding concrete blocks to the wall he was building at the front of the property. Since he was building right near our wall, he wanted to ask permission to take his wall higher than ours, explaining that it would become a covered patio. From our veranda, it appears there are three small structures contained on his property. I believe his sister and her 3 children live in the front one, he in another, and possibly other family members in the third. They mostly keep to themselves but play recordings of popular American music and old rock'n'roll, sometimes in Spanish and occasionally in English. They, like many average Hondureños in the country, live most of their days outdoors. They have hammocks and chairs set up around the yards and do their laundry and cook most of their meals outside. They often will have homemade grills, stoves or a brick oven in the yard rather than heat up the house.

A coconut tree hangs over into my yard from this neighbor's place. It regularly houses some species of bossy, black birds that scold me from the branches at intervals during the day. At first, I found it distracting to listen to; now I have learned to accept it as part of my life here. There is always some noise or other coming from the collected family and its activities. One day, that same coconut tree started giggling and whispering; that was more disturbing than the birds. I was trying to ignore it and discount the sound, but you have to admit, a giggling coconut tree is a definite distraction. I walked onto the veranda, forgetting my glasses, and peered at the tree like Mrs. Magoo, trying to locate the sound. The twenty-foot distance, without my specs, made it challenging, especially since the sound that would help me locate the source was no longer there. Eventually the whispering, and then the giggling started again. With glasses applied, I let my eyes follow the sound, and there among the fronds and foliage, I spotted a red shirt with brown arms. I put two and two together and realized that a couple of the children from the enclave had climbed the tree to pick *cocos* for their mother and their curiosity had distracted them. *"¿Hóla, Como su llama usted?"* My asking for their name brought more giggles but let them know they were spotted and reminded them of their task. They responded with *"Hóla!"* and shimmied down the tree.

The community here is social and gathers to support the *fútbol* (soccer games), pageants, and other local events. Music, whistling or singing drifts in the windows of our *casa* as the laundry is hung, as the cows are herded, or as the children play in the street. The quiet that Ordin and I desired does not exist here. There is noise, but it is from the business of living; it is not ego, not invasive. As we sit in the gazebo in the evening, listening to the sounds of the community carried on the breeze, I realize that maybe it was not quiet we were searching for but peace and harmony, which I believe we will find here.

Mahogany

Hondureños love wood and mahogany is one of their favorite hardwoods. Honduran mahogany is a rich, honey-brown color with occasional red streaks. I fell in love with mahogany when my mother bought a Duncan Phyfe dining set while I was a teenager. I had never before seen anything more beautiful, but my admiration for the wood is being re-evaluated since moving here.

The mahogany forests are protected now so we are fortunate to have so much of the wood in our house. The problem is that Hondurans have had it in their lives for so long that they are bored with it and usually stain it a deep burgundy. Our home follows Honduran style. Concrete homes, like ours, often have a ceiling molding as well as baseboard molding, and since mahogany grows here...why not use it for the moldings? When I first entered this house, I had the sensation of exceptionally high ceilings, but on measuring, I found they were just a bit over the normal eight feet. They appear to be of greater height because the builder placed the windows low, offering visibility beyond the extended roofline of the veranda. Since metal curtain rods are a rarity in this area of the country, heavy, handmade wooden curtain rods and brackets were made and hung above each window. All of this wood is stained the burgundy-red. After a time in the house, I began to feel I was walking through a geometric nightmare, with lines running ceiling and floor, down halls and around corners until my eyes met a large mahogany barrier: an oversized door. Any one of these items could be a thing of beauty but all of it was overload. Ordin's paint contracting experience is from Florida, where white and light is the core of decorating. His first instinct was to cover everything with white primer—walls, doors, woodwork and ceiling—then start from scratch. While this idea was mulling around our brains, it would invariably become part of our conversation with some of the Hondureños we were meeting. Each person would reply with mock horror, as though we were about to commit a sacrilege. No one would ever PAINT wood!

Now what do we do? What had started out as a decision was turning into a dilemma. The locals implied that true Hondureños would leave the wood, but we had not moved here to be Honduran. We wanted Caribbean, which would be light and breezy. By now, the geometric effect had become distracting and the choices felt limited to our Florida "same-o, same-o," or what felt like Honduran geometric insanity. There had to be another choice. Finally, it dawned on me: Caribbean style was an eclectic mix of materials; whatever was lying about. We should follow that theme but in our style. We could paint the ceiling molding the same color that we chose for the walls, while leaving the stained baseboards and doors as our offering to the Honduran culture. The large rooms invited bold choices in color so we selected from nature's palette. The golden sunrise of summer inspired the living room color while the entryway took center stage with the predawn purple-blue of Pico Bonito Mountain. The adjacent kitchen would quietly command its space with the clear gold color of noonday sun. The last wall visible from the main living area was the fifteen-foot hallway leading to the bedrooms. The color we chose for this space was an apricot-papaya color that would mimic sunset. While the carpenters were laying tile, we replaced the large wooden doorframes on the outside of the house with narrow, multicolored tile that incorporates most of the same colors we had chosen for inside the house. The mix of bold color, wood, and tile would give a relaxed, beach look that honored everyone's beliefs, with no hard-and-fast rules. After all, is that not what Caribbean life is all about?

Water

I am so tired of having to think about water. It is something that most folks I know take for granted, like walking; now it is something I have to be aware of and it is irksome. I can remember when my cousin lived in Puerto Rico and was vexed at the city's untimely controlling of utilities. Electricity would fail without a moment's notice and the city leaders periodically shut off the water. I remember clucking some sympathetic response and thinking, "How odd." but was truly not too concerned. I also thought, "If this is the norm, she should stay prepared for it." I do not know if I am now experiencing an act of karma, an example of the golden rule, or the result of a Hermetic law. But that conversation from years ago pops into my head each time I find myself without this simple essence of life.

Our water system is gravity fed from the city storage tank in the mountains. It is some of the purest water in the country and the locals all drink from the tap. Since bacteria in every area are different and our water is held in a ten-year-old concrete cisterna, we chose to buy drinking water in five-gallon bottles delivered to the house three times a week. The first time we ran out of water was when we miscalculated our use of purchased drinking water, but that was easily resolved by a drive to town. The second time, we ran dry in the cisterna because our house does not have an automatic fill. We had not realized this situation until the caretaker forgot to fill the cisterna tank before he went home one afternoon. He had made an effort to explain this system to us the first day we arrived but...you know...the language thing.

The cisterna is actually perfect for this area. Honduras has many mountain ranges with a good supply of rain, so letting the water naturally flow down toward the ocean is logical and affordable. Most people in El Porvenir live in ground-level homes and the water flows right to their taps under its own pressure. There may not be a lot of pressure but water bills are extremely low since there is no pumping needed. We live in a two-story home and we have a cisterna that holds about two hundred gallons. The gravity feed fills the concrete tank and a pump forces it up to the second level. As I said, it is a good system until something between the mountains and the upstairs interferes. We have been without water since yesterday afternoon when a city water pipe broke. I do not know what the other three reasons have been during our six weeks here because...you know... the language thing.

Big City

I am very content with country living. The rural atmosphere of El Porvenir feels perfect for me, but every week Ordin and I like to explore a new area of Ceiba when we travel into town for supplies. It is a town that always has a hum. The busy flow of purple-striped taxis adds to the colorful business that goes on everywhere. The city is much newer than Porvenir and planned around a town square that still acts as the hub. There are tourist information booths, and vendors offering fresh juice or souvenirs dot the space around the park, which has become a meeting place for people you know or folks that are visiting. Parking is always at a premium in town, especially this area of the busy downtown center, but if you take it slow and watch for a smile and a wave, someone will guide you to an available spot. There are always entrepreneurs who will direct you in or out of an available space...for a tip. A couple of extra Lempiras will get your car washed in its stall while you are gone to shop or run errands. Honduras does not have many laws that overprotect so an air of self-reliance develops, and since there is no public welfare system, the townspeople help support their own. Occasionally I see a blind woman guided along the street median by one of her neighbors, allowing those who are wealthy enough to be driving an opportunity to share in her support. Intersections always seem to be the ideal place to open a business, whether it is newspaper sales, having your windows washed, or children selling bags of fresh fruit.

On the side streets, cart vendors sell fresh herbs, melons, bananas, and cooked food items. A furniture shop might advertise its pieces by having them carried down the middle of the boulevard. Shoes, plastics, clothes, and toys are offered from green painted wooden stalls along the street—the general color that identifies permitted vendors. In every available space that does not block a store entrance you will find someone selling something.

Besides the colorful buildings, purple-striped taxis, and green vendor stalls, there are orange and white plastic bags...everywhere. I was amazed at the number of places that chose these bags for their customers' purchases; they seem to come in all sizes. Their popularity caused me to wonder if they, like the green vendor carts and stalls, were offered by the city. I have seen them all along this area of the coast carrying lunches, tools, rubbish, or plants, as well as new purchases. Whatever needs to be toted can be in these amazingly strong bags. We always save them to line our rubbish can and it is impossible to tear them as the trash is carried out. But I did learn there always seems to be a small hole in the bottom of each bag, a token safety factor I imagine, which makes wet garbage wrapping necessary. I finally asked the right person and found that their popularity was not only based on their strength and size, but because they are made outside Ceiba, which makes them the most affordably priced.

The Last Shipment Arrives

The last of our packages have arrived. We greeted the freight forwarder at our gates with the same anticipation reserved for a welcomed houseguest. We had been counting the days expecting this shipment. In our haste to reunite with our treasures, we helped carry the dusty, dirty boxes out of the sun and into the shelter of the carport. We signed the receipt, handed over the payment and waved good-bye to the driver as we closed the gate once more; now we were ready. With the intensity of a starving person reaching for food, Ordin and I tore the tenacious, gray duct tape from around the containers. Then, opening the first one and spotting its contents, I gleefully dug out my waterless cookware, holding each piece close to my heart. The reunion continued, but on a different note, as the three of us slowly started sifting through the packing material of the remaining boxes, carefully uncovering remnants of our former life... similar to archeologists handling ancient relics. It became a sacred time. It was the reclaiming of all the last shreds of our previous life; a reuniting. Even Pu wanted to be in the boxes, sniffing, searching, and reconnecting with the smells of what had been her home. Living without my normal household things for this long had been a humbling experience. This was the last of it. Real kitchen knives, Pu's favorite brand of tuna, and Ordin's laser level were all among the treasures we were uncovering.

In retrospect, if I had it all to do again, I believe tools and books would be the most important items to bring. Textiles of some sort can always be purchased anywhere, art is regional, but the quality tools that you are accustomed to for daily living in the kitchen, house, or yard are not always available. There have been many times since we arrived here that I felt like a twenty-first century person who has traveled through space to a less advanced point in time. It is an eerie sensation; not bad, but a subtle realization that something else exists. Other than the fundamental tools I just mentioned, the only other items I would make a priority to bring on a move like this would be the keepsakes that help you stay connected to the ones you love.

abril — April

Pintura

Just because I had chosen colors of paint for the house does not mean that painting went high on the list of priorities for improvements. Since I spent most of my time between the stale, melon-colored walls of this *casa*, I was acutely aware of little being done to change the inside. The other improvements had put such a drain on our budget that I had been willing to wait until more funds were available; however, as much as I understood the delay, I wanted some COLOR. I wanted a change! With my tolerance wearing thin, I put the pressure on Ordin for the two us to travel into La Ceiba to the paint store that had loaned me their sample book and take the first step. We bought five gallons of primer, with brushes, rollers, and an extension pole. I would start the priming myself, and when extra money was available, we would hire a painter to finish.

I started in the big main living area by coating the walls and ceiling, hoping to find a painter before it was time to prime the windows. Ordin had already done the prep work by caulking the windows, ceiling moldings, and any visible nail holes. It surprised us to find that nothing in the house, except the sinks, was sealed. Caulking compound is available in Honduras but our indicators implied that it is not in high demand. Since the climate here does not require a structure to be sealed against weather, the concept of using caulk for finishing work is more or less considered an unnecessary expense, or "*no necesario.*"

Once I had finished priming the living area AND windows, I was excited to begin applying color. The thrill of seeing new colors in the house overrode the disenchantment from days of painting, while the resolve that a painter would soon be found to finish the work kept me moving forward in my efforts. Our coastal area was into the ninety-degree temperatures of spring, so my painting attire became an old blue swimsuit worn under a pair of shorts. Dressed this way, I started painting by seven in the morning, and by noon when it had gotten too hot to do more and I was ready to stop for the day, I dove into the river for a swim before having lunch.

Days became weeks and then stretched into months. The main floor of the house has only two bedrooms and two baths, and the kitchen-living area, but the square footage measures about twenty-five hundred. Every wall and ceiling was primed first and then painted with two coats of paint. That meant painting every surface three times...if I liked the finished look. There were actually three areas where I disliked the results enough to repaint. One was the long entry wall in the living room that was intended to make a bold statement. The perfect deep-blue-purple color of the mountains was pictured in my mind even before I found it in the color swatch booklet, but when I ordered the paint, my sense of bold had waned to a pale federal blue. The finished look had all the intensity of a kiss from your sister. The second attempt at bold became a fuchsia scream and needed an extra coat of primer to void. I finally asked O to go back to the paint store one more time with a picture I had found that contained the color. He returned home carrying a can of paint that was the color I had been originally impressed to buy. The majesty that became the final finish represented an interesting lesson of faith and importance of not questioning one's intuition.

With the living area finished and no painter in sight, I began the bedrooms and hall. When I was ready to tackle the downstairs areas I was so burnt-out from painting that Ordin put out extra effort and found a painter who claimed to be a professional and could fit into our budget. He charged only three hundred Lempiras a day (about fifteen dollars U.S.). He wanted to paint the outside of the house and quoted us four hundred dollars U.S. for labor. The low price frightened me so I suggested that we see what he could do in one of the ten-by-ten-foot rooms downstairs. He indicated, in his version of "Spanglish", it would take him three days to do all that we wanted and he set a price. He spent the first day caulking and the second day priming the ceiling and four walls. Sometime during those three days he applied two coats of paint. His painting technique put so much paint on the walls the two gallons we had bought were no longer enough. Our neighbors warned us to always buy all the color that you need for a room at one time, but now we needed more. We went back to the same store and ordered another gallon of the same off-white color. It did not match the paint already on the walls and everywhere he did not reapply became obvious. Not including primer, he went through four gallons of paint. I believe he hoped to apply the paint thick enough to avoid the extra coats, but the white-on-white application was so uneven he still needed to fulfill the two-coat promise. The weekend was coming, and of course he wanted payment for the finished job, so he applied more paint the same day. Two weeks later the walls were still tacky.

He was not the professional he had claimed to be, but because we knew he needed money and did do a good caulking job, we agreed that he could do the second small downstairs room under my supervision. It went a bit better. We did not use nearly the same amount of paint, but when finished you could see where he ran the roller against the ceiling rather than cut it in. I guess he figured no one would notice since it was white against white. All the upstairs window trim that I had saved for a professional, I am now painting. My seeds of hope in finding a professional to do it have withered and died like tender seedlings in this tropical sun.

Our neighbor had her cousin from Roatan paint her house when we first arrived. As with many of the islanders, he is happy, robust, and loves to sing. We had mentioned that we wanted the outside of the house painted when we first met him and he gave us a fair price. But, after the weeks of racket from our carpenters, we had postponed the date to have this man come and live downstairs for the period of time that he would need to complete the painting. Now I have told Ordin we WILL have him come next spring to paint the house. I have seen his work—not perfect but highly acceptable—and, as a Roatanor, he speaks English...of a sort. The Roatan dialect sounds like a mix of English, Cajun, and Jamaican. We will have to negotiate meals (I do not want to cook in the evenings) and he prefers to work with oil-based paints, while we prefer water based. He had wanted five hundred dollars (U.S.) to do the entire two-story house, including all window bars. If we can stay out of his way and not interfere, maybe he can finish in ten days and be on his way back to the island while we sit and admire our home in peace.

Semana Santa

Semana Santa is Holy Week. It runs from Palm Sunday through Easter Sunday. With all the business of settling in, I was only vaguely aware that Easter was approaching. Growing up in a Protestant family and living much of my life around the conservative, middle and eastern parts of the U.S., my experience with Easter had been egg hunts, candy, a new outfit for church, and family dinner. When I asked the young mother next door how Hondureños traditionally recognize the holiday, she called it Semana Santa and vaguely mentioned an egg hunt on the beach Easter morning. She also stated that a few coastal folks go to the mountains for the week and that much of the population from the capital travels over to this side for a week at the beach. Our Porvenir beach is one of the most popular in the country, and since the community had met their goal of having the beach completely clean and cleared of debris, it was ready. It all sounded enjoyable and tame but possibly crowded. Neither of the two churches in our community had advertised special services, so Ordin and I stocked the refrigerator and planned on a quiet holiday.

With no more thought of the holiday, I put my focus and energies back to the last-minute preparations for my mid-March retreat to Mexico and the plans to visit my family afterwards. I am sure there must have been more conversation about the upcoming holiday in El Porvenir but I was busy with my own events. My travels kept me away until after the first of April. The retreat among the Mayas and along the white sand beaches of Quintanaroo had gone well, as did the visit with family in the Midwest. When I returned to the *casa* in Honduras, I noticed the enclave neighbors had been doing a bit of construction, enclosing their front structure with the support of our security wall. I was not happy with that and knew it needed to be addressed. I had asked for help from my bilingual friend just as the sister from the enclave came knocking on the front gate. It was the Friday evening before Palm Sunday. She had a carefully typed request (in Spanish) asking permission to open an all-night disco in time for the *Semana Santa* week. Holy Week was about to become more aptly named "HOLY COW!"

It seems that somewhere around the time we moved in, this neighbor went to the local *Municipalidad* to request, and was granted, a permit for a small bar. She and her brother had built a patio onto her little house at the front of the property and enclosed it with a wall, attached to ours. A small bar? Well, this explained why we heard music playing all the time. Neither Ordin nor I had realized what went on behind the other side of our wall. Had we known all this was happening, we still might not have objected since the noise had been kept to a minimum. Once I held her petition in my hands, everything changed. I may not understand many Spanish words but DISCO is universal and it is not quiet, so I knew I did not want to have it next door. When I refused to sign and told her that my lawyer would need to look at it, she became agitated and said that she would be having a disco party next week anyway. This was Friday evening and my lawyer, of course, would be gone on Saturday. Sunday was Palm Sunday and the beginning of *Semana Santa*, so all professional businesses and governmental businesses closed down for the week. Honduras has it's share of appropriate laws, but without the trained workforce, many are never enforced.

The professional sound equipment and DJ arrived the next day. We were stuck. Twenty feet from our house and bedroom windows was a disco that was open from two in the afternoon to anytime after midnight. There was no escape. All we could do was find a way to survive the week. Buses flooded the town bringing in happy beachgoers; the place was booming. Our next-door disco was competing with the music from the *cantinas* on the beach, which was also amplified for extra attention. My dairyman across the road and a couple of the other neighbors had spoken to the woman, but this was her one week to make her fortune, and her neighbors suffering was the least of her concerns. There was no one else to go to since the mayor had gone camping and the two police officers for our village were off for the week. The Army had supplied two officers to patrol only the beach. There was no use in our trying to complain; the limited amount of Spanish that we knew did not prepare us for this need. My friend, the young mother, had left town for the week to help a family member, so we had no help at all. There was nothing we could do but close the windows on that side of the house and be grateful that our bedroom had an air-conditioning unit.

It was amazing to watch the effects the booming Disco music had on our nervous systems. I spent much of the week chewing my nails and the skin around them, and a tremor developed in my right hand. Ordin began showing pink stress rings around the rims of his eyes, in part due to the lack of sleep, and Pueo was acting moody and depressed. The three of us went to bed early since the quality of life gave us no reason to want to stay up late. We covered the windows with a heavy blanket and turned on the air-conditioner in an attempt to muffle the sound enough to sleep until sometime in the early morning when quiet would signal the close of the saloon. Even with all of our efforts, we would lay in bed listening to the windows rattle while the walls and floor of our concrete house vibrated. We prayed for the predawn quiet that would offer our nerves a few hours of rest, while each morning my mind, numbed by noise and vibration, wondered with curious amazement how we had managed to survive the night. One part of me, acting as an observer of my thoughts, studied with curiosity the impressions passing through my brain as though witnessing something outside me. I remember being curious if there had been studies done on any increase in violence since the popularity of rap, and wondering at the vengeful scenarios that offered themselves for validation. By the end of the week, the fatigue and tension had played out its toll on all of us and we found ourselves on edge with each other.

Then the clouds parted, the sun rose, and it was Easter Sunday. What a beautiful, tranquil morning. In the gentle quiet of the morning, a distant church moderately broadcast its music by loudspeaker. The peace of the morning continued through the late morning and stretched into early afternoon. About one o'clock in the afternoon, the disco monster tried to raise its ugly head again but faded, finally surrendering an hour later to the peace of the ascension. A mass exodus of buses could be seen leaving Porvenir, filled with partiers returning to their homes. The discordant disco assault was over and we had survived. We would have tranquility in our lives again, but would we ever be the same? On Monday, we planned to make the appointment to take our frayed nerves to the lawyer to insure that this never happened again.

piña jugo

I was working at the computer in the late morning, trying to get caught up on e-mail that had come during one of our internet downtimes. Ordin was involved with a project, don César was quietly working in the garden, and Rosanna was busy in the kitchen. She has been part of our family for a month and she seems to have her responsibilities and the routine down pat, so I just let her do what she feels necessary without much supervision. Soon she was standing at my shoulder, holding out a glass of golden liquid, questioning,

"*¿Piña?*" She had brought a pineapple to the house just a day or two before and given it to us. After graciously thanking her, I placed it on the kitchen counter. Ordin and I had just eaten a pineapple the previous day and felt it was enough cone fruit to suit our cravings for a while. While Rosanna's gift sat unattended for those two days, I am sure she became concerned that we gringos do not know what to do with them and that it would spoil, so she made juice. It was like nothing I had ever tasted before—absolutely delicious. The flavor was not overly sweet, not heavy or filling, but truly refreshing. It was nothing like the container beverage.

April must be the season for pineapples in Honduras because three days later don Cesár brought us two more. They were the most picture-perfect fruit I had ever seen—in the peak of ripeness. In our practiced Spanish, we commented on the size and beauty of the fruit, then thanked him graciously and carried them inside. I placed them on the same space of kitchen counter where the other had been so Rosanna would see them and incorporate them into the weekly menu. I can only assume that since she did not bring these, she was not as concerned with their spoiling, as three days later they were still in the same area of the counter where I had left them. Knowing no other way to approach the subject, I picked up one of them and asked her, "*¿Porfavor, para jugo?*"—for juice, please?

I had not seen Rosanna make the beverage earlier and I was curious how she had accomplished it. The only juicer we had was my grandmother's old, electric, citrus squeezer. Since I did not remember hearing a machine, nor could I imagine how she would get a pineapple on the old appliance, I hung around the kitchen to observe. She skillfully moved through the basic preparation of washing the fruit and cutting away the top, and then the astounding process began. Rosanna started to squeeze the fruit. She began with only the top three to four inches in a motion that was somewhere between kneading and choking, then she worked her way around the fruit, the strength of her fingers rivaling that of the strongest massage therapist. When the fruit filled with the needed liquid, she poured off the juice and repeated the process. Once she had extracted all she could from that depth, she took the same knife that had topped the fruit and began to dig out the flesh to expose the lower level. The procedure would repeat for the bottom portion. With my eyes glued to her hands I watched the process unfold. The scenario taking place before me vividly portrayed the story I had heard of a young girl taken out of school to work all-day in the hot pineapple fields to help support her family. The keen piece of German cutlery this same girl now used would have then been a machete, the only utensil the child carried into the fields. With experience, it became a multipurpose tool and the fruit she cultivated or picked was her source of energy and refreshment. The skill I was witnessing came from many years and tears. It also reinforced that this was a country of cheap labor, so there was no incentive to employ expensive, laborsaving equipment.

I often look out at don César working in the yard and wonder at the routine he has set up for himself. The love and labor he invested in this property has created a botanical paradise. Leaves and spent blossoms are raked from the yard every morning. His machete found many uses, from edging the gardens and walks, to pruning shrubs and harvesting coconuts for us. The complicated systems for maintenance that had become necessary dumbfounded Ordin and me, many of which resulted from the reluctance to invest in materials when labor was so cheap. Yet, even with the intensity of labor needed to perform each task, Rosanna and don César's temperaments always seem pleasant. These chores are considered part of life.

Most Honduran people are so agreeable and friendly the first impulse in these situations is to pay higher wages, but Oscar had told us this was not the solution. Fast, easy money can be the downfall of a society, so when we wrote our original contract, we chose to pay the high-end of the accepted pay scale and reduce the hours a day that our staff worked. We also invested in quality tools for them to use to perform their work and made long-needed repairs to household systems. We wanted to be sensitive to the self-respect associated with working hard but plant seeds of change that might allow for another way. Who could have realized the insight that came with that glass of juice? I will never see *piña jugo* the same way again.

The Marañon Tree

A large tree grows beside our house; no one that I can speak with can tell me how old it is. I was told that before the wall and before the house, when there was only an empty pasture leading to the river, there was the marañon. Its effect on onlookers is mesmerizing, with its huge trunk bending, twisting and sprawling from the earth to the lofty heights that overlook the roof of our house. A Bonsai master could not have shaped a more artistic pose. It gracefully drapes across our wall, as though having a neighborly chat with the young mother next door while watching the activity in her yard. It is like the grand matriarch of the neighborhood. It feeds, shelters, and houses freely. *Marañon* is Cashew. Its flowers supply the bees in February; its yellow fruit feeds the birds through April, May and June, while its shade protects all. The colorful array of birds that fills the tree is as varied as splashes from an artist's palette. The fruit of this tree is sweeter than mango and considered a delicacy. Neighbors used to gather it while their children collected the seedpods of the withered fruit to roast on flat stone plates until the hard shells surrendered their tasty treasure. Then, ten years ago, someone bought the property, built a house, and sealed themselves from the neighborhood with two large metal gates. Subsequently, what everyone had shared became the property of one. The *marañon* tree and the river were no longer the casual access of the folks that lived in the *barrio*.

Our dining area has a glass extension that runs from ceiling to floor, and Mother *Marañon* grows just outside this windowed space. I am creating a garden room in that spot that offers me the sensation of sitting up in her bough, almost like being in a tree house, sharing space with the yellow birds and parrots. This is one of my favorite areas of the house. Witnessing how the tree changes with each season has given me more understanding of some research Ordin had done before we ever left Hawai'i. Some of our friends there had one of these trees on their property, and since we love the nuts we were intrigued. However, the more we researched and read, the less interested we became in having a tree like that on our property. It just seemed that the rare nut was not worth all the trouble. In three months, I have become a convert from research to experience. I have found that nurturing by a *marañon* is a privilege.

The benevolence of the *marañon* amazes Ordin and me as we have watched its progression. While the birds work the branches, the fruit falls prolifically, supplying a generous prize twice a day. Rosanna has rewarded us with fresh juice made from the fruit, the taste of which brings to mind the word "ambrosia." The frailty of the fruit causes it to be so luxuriant that it is considered a reward to anyone who comes to the house. When area children know we are approachable, they will ask to scour the ground for the hard shells and the fruit. It is such a thrill to share our discovery and there has been more than enough for each neighbor to share in the abundance.

Even Pueo has developed an appreciation for the spreading limbs. She climbs the huge branches to observation points that allow her to study the neighbor's caged parrots from a safe and sheltered distance. Time and again, the young mother and I will chat from one house to the other, she from her small veranda that faces my house, while I stand at the open Zen door. This habit makes Pu and Ordin a bit uneasy, but I brace my foot at the doorsill and feel perfectly safe. One evening Pueo came to the open Zen door where I stood talking. As she looked down to the ground below, her reaction was to try to coax me inside since she does not like the view. This time she withdrew and left the house through her cat window, going down the stairs to the ground below. I was unaware that she was no longer at my side until the flowering vine at the base of the cashew tree started to quiver. Then, a dark streak shot up the tree; it was Pu. She did not stop at the parrot observation point but continued two limbs higher until her elevation was even with our heads. There she sprawled on one of the limbs, ready to join the visit. She was one of the girls, and even if she had nothing to say, she and Mother *Marañon* would keep their eyes on us.

Mum's the Word

I am pissed! I have not had internet access for two weeks. I cannot get to the post office in Ceiba. Hondutel, the local phone service, came through last week to sign up folks who wanted their service. I have a phone number now, but no telephone service. The only person I can call on my cell phone is Ordin, and since I am directing most of my frustration at him, it would result in a negative burning of my cell minutes. Communication continues to be the major challenge here. If it is not my stumbling through trying to speak the language, it is phones or internet. I believe that I am working my way through the Personal Growth alphabet with each transition of my life. Florida was A-Achievement, Hawai'i was learning B-Balance, now C-Communication in Honduras. I am curious about the next step...it should be a D. Let me see...Devious? Delicious? Doubting? Delirious? Desirous! Probably something dull like Devoted.

I spend most of my time writing so I am not getting to practice communicating in *español* as much as Ordin, who is working with don Cesár and some of the local men who do our day labor. Necessity is the mother of...skill, in this particular case. Each morning when don Cesár comes to work, he greets us with his English greeting of "Good morning, Malana. How are you?" He has been practicing English from some television shows and the neighbor children who learn it in school. Sometimes he will sit and have coffee with us before his workday begins and quiz me on the Spanish words that he has been trying to teach me. He and Ordin both enjoy my floundering as I destroy the language, trying to recall the correct word for rock or rain.

I was fatigued and burnt-out when we left Hawai'i. Phone calls and appointments from people with sick parents, children, marriages that were failing; all these people needing help. One of my friends from the mainland gave me the Native American name "Pachamama" when she saw how people came or called. I remember stating that I did not want to talk to anyone for a month after we made the move to Honduras. Well, it has been three months. Now I want to talk to my daughter, I want to hear from my friends, I want to know what is happening to my Hawai'i 'ohana. Will this ever get easy? Will we ever have a smooth system in which to connect our old life to this new one?

I never realized how difficult it had to be for foreigners coming to the U.S. No wonder they seek out people of their own nationality with whom to spend their time. The language, the customs, the fear of not understanding the laws, finding a birthday card, wanting to say hello to your neighbors or trying to understand your way around town; it all just seems so hard. Part of this frustration comes from wanting to do what I want to do somewhere near the time I want to do it. Then, as I lay in bed at night with all these thoughts running through my head, craving contact with familiar people, somewhere in the neighborhood someone has put on music—beautiful music. I cannot understand a word of the lyrics. But as the breezes from the Caribbean carry its melody into my room and across my body, it quiets my mind, caresses my nerves, and I fall asleep knowing everything will work out.

mayo — May

¡Calor!

It is hot! April and May, including June until the solstice, are the hot summer months for this North Coast. It is a dry, intense heat. Every conversation with anyone we meet includes two words I can always understand: "*¡Mucho Calor!*" When we left Hawai'i, one of the discomforts we were leaving was the cool dampness of our area. Our kids would call from the mainland and tell us of the heat waves and droughts in their areas and we would be in Hawai'i, wearing long sleeves in the morning. We were ready for some heat.

We do not have a thermometer or a television so we can only guess the Fahrenheit. The temperature feels like it's in the mid-to-high 90°s, and the wonderfully cool Caribbean breezes have taken a vacation. There has been no rain for a month, we are watering the lawn with river water and still the grass is showing stress. I brought seeds back from my family trip into the Midwest so I could enjoy leafy salad mix, a produce unheard-of here. Within a week of planting, the only leaves that broke the soil were the ones in the back of the garden — a section that is in the all-day shade. The ground is too hot for seeds now. I started some tomato seeds in little peat cubes to see if they can grow in pots placed under small trees around the yard. Don Cesár and I are very interested in this *experimento*, he having never seen formed peat containers before and me hoping for a homegrown tomato.

Our relief comes from the water. A dip in the river, just outside our rear gate, is the most refreshing experience I can think of during the heat of summer. Plunging into its cool depths gives immediate relief from the heat of the day and feeds the spirit with the beauty of the surrounding area. Whether sitting on the pier or becoming one with the gentle current, a glance in either direction can cause a shift of your senses. Gazing upriver, the overhanging canopy of jungle vegetation creates a tunnel effect, drawing your spirit deeper and deeper into a place that feels lost in time. All awareness becomes stilled as man and nature become one under the watchful eyes of de

Nombre de Dios, "The Name of God" mountain range. As I turn my head to face the mouth of the river, the thrill of the surreal floods over me as I find myself at eye level with the breaking waves of the Caribbean Sea less than three hundred yards away. The spiritual oneness with the *rio* is often short-lived since the river is also a popular place for the area youngsters to swim. Ordin and don Cesar repaired our pier and built a ladder, which has almost promoted our dock to resort status according to the local kids. From our veranda we often hear children laughing and splashing at the dock throughout the afternoon. Occasionally, adults haul plastic chairs to the piers to sit and visit while the children play, and the shift from day to darkness helps produce the light breezes that offer a reprieve from the heat of the day. Those who wish more activity head for the beach. The cool, fresh, ocean waves supply a refreshing break between volleyball, basketball, beachcombing, or snoozing. And for those who cannot decide between saltwater and fresh, where the river and ocean join they have formed an alliance to create a brine pool that meets the needs of all ages.

My first evening to drive through town was an education on the community at night. Almost everyone who does not have a porch facing the main thoroughfare was out walking the streets. It was an eerie feeling as we approached this scene, since my first impression was a flashback to a zombie movie from my childhood. The movie had depicted lifeless people slowly moving out of the darkness and wandering the streets. After this first notion, my eyes and the more logical left side of my brain became aware of mothers carrying babies, children playing in the roads, and men standing around talking. Every person was taking advantage of the evening breezes while they waited for their homes to cool enough to sleep. Ordin and I have not tried to join this society since we still struggle communicating and we have the luxury of an air-conditioner in our bedroom. When the evening darkness finally signals the time for us to go inside, we drop the shades, turn on the air-conditioner and pop in a DVD. Our large bedroom easily becomes a studio apartment and life becomes comfortable again. I sprawl in my PJs, snacking on fruit, watching English-speaking movies, and letting my air-conditioner erase the distance between where I am and the life I knew.

Red and Black Rings

It was evening. We have a "Happy Hour" custom of walking outside with Pueo. This began in Hawai'i and Pu has clung to it through all the trauma of the move and relocation. About five o'clock in the evening she will come to let us know the neighborhood is quiet, the winds have calmed to gentle breezes and the heat of the day is past. It is time to lock the gates and play in the grass together.

Ordin and I take a *cervesa* or a glass of *vino* to sip as we stroll around the lawn, while Pu menaces the birds and does her personal business. It is a chance for the three of us to release the trials of the day and share the joys while we stalk and play with Pu. It is a special time for all of us and we will often linger around the yard and gazebo until after dark. Since Ordin framed a cat door for Pu in one of the living room screens, we have been able to let her remain outside alone as much as she likes in the evening, coming inside when we call her for bed.

It was getting close to that time for us. Ordin and I were in our nightclothes, propped in bed watching one of our DVDs, when I thought I heard Pu calling. This was not one of her normal "come keep me company" whines; it was a strange call—insistent—and it was coming from within the house. Worried, I left the room to search the house; she sounded nearby. I groped for the light switches as I made my way down the hall, apprehensive about what I might find. Suddenly, I spotted her under the dining table; she had something hanging from her mouth. I assumed she caught something and wanted to show us. It did not look like a lizard or an insect. "Damn! Where are my glasses, anyway?" I mumbled. As I dropped to my knees to get a closer look in the dim light under the table, Pu spit her catch out on the floor and stepped back. A snake! It was a snake with red and black rings! It has been years since I have seen one but I thought, "That is a coral snake!" Pueo laid on the cool terrazzo, watching and waiting to see what I would do with this thing. As a Hawai'i cat, she has never known snakes; her experience is limited to lizards, birds and rodents

The young mother had just mentioned, when we talked earlier that day, that we were into the season for snakes. She explained why her husband had cut one of the limbs of the cashew tree: it had reached the edge of their roof, which could allow snakes access to the attic. When the weather is hot and dry and the *marañon* fruit is dropping to the ground, the coral snakes come out in the coolness of night. The awareness of snakes had become a thing of my past once we moved to the islands. While living in the Ozarks, it was just a part of life to realize that I shared the outdoors with snakes and other critters, and even Florida had its dangerous reptiles. It was a simple matter of training to be in the present and not put any of your body parts into places reputed to house reptiles.

Nevertheless, here it was—a snake. Pueo was waiting to see what we should do with it. I often catch and release her trophies but I did not want this one brought back into the house, and it was important to teach her that it was *malo*, or "bad". I tried calling Ordin for backup but he could not hear me over the movie. The jaws of the snake were gnashing about, trying to locate something to lock its teeth into, but so far it had not tried to leave. I made a dash to the kitchen and opened the utensil drawer, grabbing the first handle I found in the mayhem of cutlery. It was the famous Ginsu knife; it would do the job. On my return, the snake was no longer under the table; it had begun to travel. I spotted Pueo tracking it but staying a safe distance behind. Within seconds of reaching them, the snake's head lay severed from the body, its jaws still grinding. I would save the remnants to show to don Cesar in the morning; he would be able to confirm my instincts. I gave Pu a rewarding scratch and went back to the bedroom where Ordin, oblivious to the life-and-death struggle that had just occurred, was snacking on cheese and still absorbed in the movie.

Spring Festival

It had been pretty quiet in the neighborhood after the end of April but the disco situation had not been completely resolved with the end of *Semana Santa*. We had tried to contact our lawyer but family health problems caused his Easter absence to extend to the end of the April. After delaying as long as we felt we could, we finally filed a formal complaint with the Porvenir Municipal. The officials were sympathetic but wanted to protect us from having an irate neighbor. They explained the disco had been operating under a temporary permit, which would expire on the twenty-ninth of the month, and asked for our patience. Without their intervention, there was no other choice. The rental of the disco's gigantic sound equipment had ended so at least the volume of noise had been significantly reduced. We sat out the remaining ten days, waiting and praying for our lawyer's return.

As it was, the two events occurred simultaneously; even so, we knew it was important to follow through with our appointment. We had stated our concern when we originally contacted the law office, so our attorney was aware of the situation when we met on the first Monday morning in May. He greeted us with a handshake and good news. His research had discovered a Law of Social Consequences, written two years before, that addressed disturbing or invasive behavior. He then traveled to El Porvenir's municipal building with a copy of the law and a letter that said they must enforce it. It has been fairly *tranquilo* ever since.

The loud music will now shift to Ceiba since it is the time of Spring Festival and Carnival. The *Fiesta de San Isidro*, takes place every year in La Ceiba in honor of the city's patron saint. The festivities rival the Mardi Gras of New Orleans and Rio de Janeiro's Carnival, without any of the bawdiness. People travel here every May from all points of the globe to participate in this weeklong event with its lavishly costumed parades, dusk-to-dawn music, and street dancing. Hondureños love a celebration and Spring Festival is one of the best; music and noise are just a part of it.

Everyone was talking about *Festivál*, even our lawyer. We learned that each of the neighborhoods, or *barrios*, puts on their own parade and party and he encouraged us to attend his area's function. Ordin and I are not fond of crowds, and having not fully recovered from the terrors of *Semana Santa*, we had considered skipping this first year of *Festivál*. Now, with this invitation, we needed to at least attend that one evening. The young mother was another who had been buzzing about the festivities but for quite another reason: her daughter had been selected to be part of the Queen's court. She told us about the processional parade in which all the court attendees from this year and last would take the mile-and-a-half walk from the beach area to the downtown square. At the south side of the square, outside the old church, there would be a crowning ceremony, ethnic dancing, fireworks, and music. She stated that she would watch for us. It all sounded colorful and vibrant, but the lure of our tranquil evening customs was causing us to look for excuses: Ordin had eaten something that was not sitting well...Pueo does not go outside until about time to leave...it was so hot, too. Suddenly, the gate next door opened and the young mom and her family were rushing to get the last of their items and return to the opening parade. She stopped to yell a greeting. Ashamed that I had been caught, I pleaded confusion over locating the parade as my justification for not having already left to join the festivities. She explained again the parade had started at six and the crowning would not take place until eight. She added that we still had time to make it if we got ready right away. We were stuck.

Spruced up and loaded into the Sport, we were on our way to Ceiba by six-thirty. Sometimes it just takes a bit of motivation. One of the things we had dreaded about attending the festivities was the aggravation of finding a parking space that would not require a taxi ride. As it was, parking is not a problem when you live in an area where public transportation is the norm. We arrived with plenty of time to park on the west side of the square and walk to Pizza Hut for a beer and light supper. We hoped that our seats at a window would let us see when the parade approached; as things turned out, the parade passed right in front of our eyes. It was absolutely perfect; we had parking, air conditioning, beer, and front-row seats.

The information I heard leading up to this event had been a bit confusing to me. Most of the people we knew talked about *Festivál*, but everywhere there was chatter and evidence of a *Carnivál*. While we sat watching the parade, and later walking with the parade, the random bits and pieces of information began to process in my mind, creating a clearer picture. Now I understood why the large fairground had been constructed outside of town; it was for the *Carnivál*. Instead of being in conflict with the *Festivál*, as I had seen in my mind, it was a complement to the event.

The opening night festivities that we were witnessing surround the Festival Queen and her court. The basis for the careful selection of these four young women is their moral standards, intelligence, and knowledge of their country's history and culture. They wore beautiful gowns and represented the Spanish Catholic heritage that surrounds Saint Isidro, the patron saint of agriculture. There was a fifth young woman, wearing the skimpiest of beaded coverings and a huge headdress, whose place in the procession indicated a status of that just below or equal to the festival queen. She, just as carefully selected, represents the Honduran Indian roots and her position was Carnival Queen. I found it interesting the homage paid to the patron saint of crops allowed for both the spiritual aspect as well as the more base side of humanity. I also noted that "religious" outnumbered "earthly" by four to one.

By the end of the week, this Queen's court had taken part in every parade in each of the *barrios* and was gearing up for the Grande Final. This is the only daytime parade and so allowed for the participation of an amazing display of equestrian breeding and skills. Hondureños' pride in their horses and riding skills runs deep in their veins, from the time of the Spanish Conquistadors. The attendance of these horses in the parade also announced the following day's horse show. However, for this moment these riders and their steeds, mixed with bands, floats, and gowns, were all lavishly decorated. Then everything is punctuated by vendors of souvenirs, toys, and food, creating one of the best parades I have ever attended.

The Massage

I am going for a massage. One of the things I appreciate most about the natural health field is the knowledge that massage is not a luxury; it is an essential part of good health. A quality massage also offers a wonderful relaxation, so no matter where we live, I find a good massage therapist and make every effort to go regularly. My neighbor recommended Elsa's.

When I arrived at *Elsa's Clinica de Masajes*, its location impressed me. It was across the street from the beach, with the ocean breezes blowing through its jalousie windows; this was a good start. Elsa, an attractive-looking, middle-aged woman with a gentle smile, spoke only a couple of words of English but she directed me to a room with a massage table and gestured that I should remove all of my clothes. This was no different from anywhere in the U.S.; generally the therapist leaves the room while the client disrobes and lays on the massage table, where there is always a light covering for modesty. Elsa left the room but returned before I managed to position myself on the table. My delay in being prone was due to being distracted by searching for the light modesty covering. There I stood, absolutely naked, while Elsa, not making eye contact, gestured that I should now lie face up on the table. At this time of my life, approaching my fifty-eighth birthday and being the grandmother of five, a protest seemed unnecessary. Obviously, bodies were nothing new to Elsa. I decided that if she could take it, then so could I. In a moment I was situated on the table and Elsa mysteriously materialized a towel, which she laid on my tummy. It was the size of a kitchen dishtowel. As she turned to get her lotion, I took the opportunity to quickly spread this scant piece of fabric, trying to cover my pubic area and breasts. With my frame being almost five-foot eight, distributing the inadequate piece of material was a challenge. The hem of the cloth just barely missed my nipples, which were proving uncooperative by lying just beyond the reach of each tiny corner. As Elsa turned from her task, my struggles proved in vain since she whisked the towel from my tummy to tuck it between my thighs.

The massage technique was also different from any I had ever experienced. Instead of long, gliding strokes, her thumbs and fingers were making a pinching motion along the length of my muscles; not completely uncomfortable, but unusual. After she was satisfied with an area, she finished with a cupped "slapping" motion along the massaged limb; again, not uncomfortable, but unusual. I closed my eyes to surrender my body to Elsa's pinching fingers, wondering if I would ever visit her establishment again. I bid my mind to quiet, reserving judgment until the end of the session. I had drifted off into a half-dream state when "Turn over." jolted me alert like a cannon blast going off beside the table. My eyes flew open; there was Elsa's face, beaming with pleasure at her ability to communicate the intent to work on my posterior. After the second half of the session, when Elsa had left the room and I was sliding back into my clothing, I began to realize that I was feeling a state of bliss or at least a wonderful sense of well being. I am not sure that I have ever truly had this feeling before, and those are the only words I can think of to describe the sensation of "joy of life" that I experienced immediately after, and for the three days following my treatment.

Now I am intrigued with a fat reduction program that she has developed. She did her best to gesture and tried to explain each of the procedures to me as we walked through the steps together. One of the treatments involves time spent in a sauna in the rear of her shop. It is a nice little sauna, not much different from any other I have used except for the barnyard sounds that emanate from the rear of the structure. Its outside wall partitions it from a neighboring yard where some clucking hens, a rooster, dog, and pig reside. The price of the one-hour massage was only one hundred eighty Lempiras, roughly ten dollars U.S.; the fat reduction plan would be about five times as much for six sessions. Will I ever return to Elsa's? I believe so. I think the time spent in the sauna alone, would be worth the price of the treatment.

Compost

May, with its accompanying heat, is almost over. From what I understand, the heat and intense sun will continue until shorter days begin after the June Solstice. The flowers in the yard never lose their vibrancy but the lifespan of each blossom seems much shorter due to the intensity of the sun. Don Cesár's daily practice of watering lessens the severity but to combine heat and moisture is fertile ground for the other plague of summer: fungus.

I have always loved to garden, even as a child, and for a few years I was a commercial grower; chlorophyll has probably stamped its imprint into my DNA. Since moving here, however, I generally let Cesár do what he does so well as I have never gardened so low in the tropics; I watch and learn from the master. Occasionally I make a suggestion when I see room for improvement, and the need for compost was one of these. When we first arrived in February, while walking the yard during the morning with Pueo, I saw many indications the soil was poor. In exchanges with don Cesár and my own soil test, I found that commercial growing had created a condition complicated by the spring flooding: chemicals were spread and topsoil was lost. All that remained was clay, sand and gravel. Since flowers and shrubs have always grown in the area, Hondurans expect them to continue to do so. Fertilizer is never collected from animals locally and chemical fertilizer is expensive, so seldom used. Our grounds still suffered from construction debris, while Cesár's daily raking removed anything that might offer nourishment to the soil. He had told me some of the history of the yard, pointing out that not much money had been spent on necessary chemicals for insects and fungus. I, in turn, tried to explain that healthy plants do not become prey to these pests as often, but I could tell I was not getting through. Ordin and I went online and found an article on composting. In the States it would be a simple matter of buying the sacked elements we needed from a discount store or garden center; here there was no market, so...compost.

The article we found went into detail on different ways to erect a compost bin plus what materials would compost well. It addressed moisture, density and PH. The information was excellent, but in English. Ordin had installed a translator program on the computer so he was able to print the instructions in Spanish for Cesár. We *habla* a bit more Spanish than we *comprende*, so we are never sure how accurately the translator works. We used this same approach with a chicken and pineapple recipe for Rosanna a couple of months ago and have yet to see anything resembling its description cross our plates. Therefore, as we handed the translated compost information to Cesár to take home and read, it was a test of faith.

Nothing was ever mentioned about the article, so Ordin and I pulled some masonry blocks together to form a bin and he fashioned a cover for it. We told don Cesár to put all the yard sweepings into the bin each day and to wet it down each Saturday. Another way to fill the compost pile quickly was to locate the "trimming man." He is a local guy who owns a weed whacker and hires out to clear small, grassy areas. I periodically see him riding his bicycle, with weed eater tied the length of the bike, going from one job to another. One day during our project, I saw him working an area around the corner from our place. He had two, neatly raked piles of clippings. A short conversation supplied me with the information I wanted, as well as the two piles of clippings. He was more than happy to give them to the crazy gringo lady; it would save him from having to cart them away. I am sure that he and Cesár had an interesting conversation as they loaded our wheelbarrow, and don Cesár obediently carried other people's yard garbage into his beautiful, botanical garden. Nevertheless, I returned home to find the compost pile filled to the brim. Scanning the collection, Ordin saw the large leaves that Cesár often rakes would call for shredding with our lawn mower if the pile was going to break down with any speed. Other than that, if we could keep it damp enough, the tropical sun would do the rest.

Here we were, three-and-a-half months later. I had topped off some potted Dieffenbachia after transplanting, and stuck the cuttings in a moist medium to root. Now it was time to plant them. Don Cesár was delighted with the *experimento* of rooting plants in styrofoam shipping pellets since Hondurans love to find a use for rubbish. I pointed out the ideal location for the young plants and he started digging a hole. The place I selected was one of the areas containing construction debris, so the dirt was a mix of shattered concrete and rock. Cesár would have normally hauled that dirt back to the river and then dug enough off the riverbank to replace it; less debris but just as much clay. This time I had him bring the wheelbarrow of dirt back to the ignored compost bin in the rear of the yard. He and I lifted the heavy lid and dug down under the dry, top layer to bring up the rich, decayed humus. Cesár immediately recognized it as being similar to the rich soil from the jungles of his youth. As I mixed the compost into the wheelbarrow of poor dirt, a transformation occurred...in the dirt and in don Cesár. He became overjoyed. Thrilled with the results he could see, he also realized it was something he knew he could do. This simple process could save the soil of his farm, let him grow vegetables at his home and improve his fruit trees. His obvious delight with this new knowledge brought tears to my eyes.

Cesár spent the morning emptying and mixing all the compost into the gardens along the wall. He was anxious to begin the next three-month crop. Ordin and I watched from our lookout on the veranda as this happy man was magically transforming soil. While we watched, we discussed the similarities of raising children and communicating with people whose language is not your own and whose lifestyles are simpler. Each of us wished we could have had the patience and skills we were developing now while we were raising our children. The language difference requires patience on our part, as well as theirs, while we work through ways to communicate. How many times, as I raised my children, did I lose patience because we could not understand each other? Age differences also cause language difficulties.

If the folks who work for us break something, they will clean it up but they cannot afford to replace it. We must replace or repair it. Ordin will never forget the day Rosanna was cleaning the window screens. She was removing the aluminum-framed screens from the windows, washing them with a wet cloth and stacking them until all were completed and ready to be replaced. He had been only vaguely aware of her project since he was busy with his own, until she came to his workroom to borrow his carpenter's hammer. Moments later he heard the heavy, metal tool striking something...not wood. Window screen! That was his first thought as he raced up the stairs to where he found Rosanna trying to beat a warped aluminum frame with sagging mesh screen back into place. Like so many people that live outside the cities, she does not have screens on the windows of her house. It must be just as great a challenge for her to learn our lifestyle as for us to understand hers. Who would have thought to consider screens an advanced idea, like...a compost pile.

Paper Products

My awareness of paper started when I wanted to write a letter and had no stationery. I looked for what I had accepted all my life as a common commodity in every shop I knew in La Ceiba, with no success. A nagging sensation in the back of my mind told me there had been the vague awareness of this void when we shopped for don Cesar's birthday card in March. Nothing had changed. There are no card shops or stationery shops here. Over the months, I have found that greetings for birthdays, anniversaries and a few other occasions can be found at the supermarket or a couple of department stores, but a handwritten letter must be a lost art at this end of the globe. School supplies are the big market here. If all I wanted was lined paper or a spiral notebook, I could buy those without ever leaving Porvenir. Each time I make a trip to the U.S., I have the intent to stock up on pretty stationery, but invariably the more immediate desire for Roman shades, double-threaded concrete screws, or a wooden elongated toilet seat challenges the priorities in my limited luggage space. The only tradeoff for this compromise is the fun of watching the expressions of the T.S.A. inspectors while they search my baggage.

This limited supply of paper products does not end with elective writing material. The expense involved with paper causes "giveaways" to be viewed as a luxury rather than a necessity. I have yet to find a paint store that has color sample sheets to give away. It is customary to sit in the store and go through color sample books like sewing pattern books in the U.S. I was referred to one shop that allowed me to take their sample color palette home for the weekend; I bought all my paint from them. Some other limits of paper that I was not accustomed to included paper napkins: they are very thin and are meted out one per entrée; and business cards. These are an investment given out sparingly to business prospects, not broadcast for advertising as is often seen in the States. Is one use better than the other? It is hard to say. I, for my part, like the one-on-one personal contact, but I have learned to ask for a card.

One other aspect of the Hondureño's perspective on paper should interest people of all ages; that is toilet paper. The septic systems in Mexico and Central America are quite small and inefficient for volumes of toilet tissue. When using these facilities in homes or public places, there is a waste can stationed beside the commode for disposal of used tissue. The exceptions to this rule are in Western developed properties or American-built homes and businesses. Americans insist on efficient waste disposal and are willing to pay the price for it.

One Sunday, Ordin and I decided to spend the day exploring the Mega Mall Plaza in Ceiba. It had been our custom to simply dash into one store or the other when we knew they carried something we needed, but we had never taken the time to explore all that was offered. It was a wonderful day, free from time constraints, to poke and peek into each of the stores on both floor levels. We met some friends from Porvenir and decided to go with them to the food court for something to drink and eat. After several beverage refills, it was time for the *señoras* to migrate to the *baño* to use the facilities. As we entered the public bathroom of the mall, my only concern was to find an empty stall and relieve the significant pressure on my bladder. Entering the first available space, I heard my friend call out, "There's no toilet paper." I looked at the roll dispenser in my stall and found, to my amazement, that she was correct. Mystified over my friend's psychic abilities, my mind vacillated between that thought and the problem: no TP. Then the image of the travel-size packet of facial tissues stashed in my purse flashed through my mind. I had needed to have these when visiting my father during my last trip to the U.S. and once again they came to my rescue. So, the problem at hand had been resolved and I was free to return to my friend to satisfy my curiosity about the source of her knowledge.

In answer to my question, she smiled and pointed her finger toward the entrance of *la mujer baño*. There, hanging on the wall next to the door, I saw two large, round, toilet tissue dispensers...empty. My puzzled look and further probing uncovered the sordid history of pilfered paper and the resolution to keep dispensers under the watchful eye of the mall maintenance. The value of toilet tissue has elevated its status on the coveting list of enough folks in Central America that this creative measure was designed. Thankfully, I had pocket tissues with me that day and from now on will always consider them as essential as my passport when leaving home.

junio — June

An Attitude of Gratitude

It is June and, just as though all of nature saw the calendar page turn, the atmosphere has changed. The stagnant heat of the last two months disappeared as mysteriously as it arrived, replaced by cool breezes and evening showers. Ordin and I were out before breakfast, driving east of Ceiba to the Sambo Creek area where one of the Garifuna villages lies, to inspect some residential construction in a new development. As we made the turn to leave our El Porvenir community, Pico Bonito Mountain loomed before us — an awesome sight, clear and uncompromised by haze or clouds. This view was my reward for caving in under Ordin's pressure to get me out of Porvenir for a large part of the day. The drive was his way of helping clear off some of the smog surrounding me.

I had kept close to home for the last two months, busy with painting, gardening with Cesár, and writing. Ordin and I had enrolled in the Central American Spanish School a week before. This forced me out of my asylum three hours a day, three days a week, but my struggles over conjugating verbs and correct articulation were adding to my list of current frustrations. Just the day before, my discouraged young professor had challenged me to explain how I could have been in the country for four months and learned so little "survival" Spanish. I explained to him that I live in a community of farmers, fishermen, and dairymen. Their conversations had taught me the words that are essential to their lives — words like *lluvia* for rain, *aire* for breeze, *vaca* for cow and *caca* for fertilizer. "Shit! They taught you to say shit?" was his shocked, wide-eyed outburst. Within moments, his composure regained, he stated that ladies (implying especially one of my age), would use the word *exctermenta*, or something that sounded like that. It was very disconcerting to be scolded by someone just a bit older than my eldest grandson. In retaliation, I decided that since I see my professor only three hours a day, three times a week, but see Cesár and my neighbors every day, I would consider keeping *caca* in my El Porvenir vocabulary. But I would remember to mumble something that sounds like the other word when I visit the plant nursery or shop the agricultural *tienda*.

My greatest frustrations have been directed at myself since many of the situations I allow to annoy me are the same, recurring problems that I deal with periodically: communication, internet, and the need to practice soooo much patience. Another point of concern was my rapidly approaching visa deadline. I needed to return to the U.S. for a few days but was torn between seeing clients in Florida and wanting to see family in Missouri. Each nagging situation was a distraction from clear thinking, much like being pecked to death by a flock of ducks. Is it any wonder that great spiritual gurus live alone on mountaintops? Is that the only place to find a center of peace? How can anyone keep their ducks in a row when their feet are entangled with computer cables? My reclusion within the limited world behind my eight-foot walls had allowed me to feed my small vexations into Pico Bonito size, and wisely, Ordin knew I needed to get out into a larger world to see a bigger picture.

This was a new part of the country to me. It was vast, green, rolling hills with occasional huge boulders and a few modest residential dwellings; only a few commercial structures dotted the highway as we traveled toward our destination. As I watched the countryside pass, my body began releasing the tension I had not realized it held. This was the beauty I had felt so much a part of in the Ozark and Appalachian Mountains, as well as the rain forest of Hawai'i. In this peaceful state, I began to create a gratitude list, a technique that I offer my clients to complement all levels of healing. I began my list of blessings with:

1. Creating a situation that would fulfill a long-time desire of wanting to learn Spanish. This would be the move to Honduras AND the mixed blessing of choosing to live in a Honduran neighborhood.

2. Having Rosanna as part of our family. Her cheerful presence, appearing out of "nowhere" with freshly made juice as we return home from a hot morning dashing around La Ceiba, or while immersed in a tedious project. Her capable qualities, which allow me the freedom to do the things I want to do, while the necessities of life are still satisfied.

3. The honor of being "watched over" by Cesár. His integrity, his gentle, kind nature and protective aura allowed an environment in which we could test the waters of our new world. His gifts of freshly caught fish and yucca root from his farm filled our stomachs as his words of wisdom filled our minds; these acts of sharing were also his way of teaching.

4. The thrill of living in a mortgage-free, beautifully designed home. As I acknowledged that thought, I realized that I could not have chosen a more perfect floor plan. Our decision to live in Honduras was allowing us a lifestyle that was prohibitive in the States.

5. The luxury of no phone interruptions and limited internet demands, which allowed time to focus on my own needs; to restore and rejuvenate from years of giving to others. The situation I had perceived as an obstacle was, in essence, an opportunity...to heal.

My expanding list was temporarily halted by our arrival at Mango Tree Villas. This property was under development by the same real estate agent who had handled the purchase of our home. While Ordin was busy inspecting vent stacks, I leaned against the car, shaded by a huge mango tree, while absorbing the view. It was refreshing to see a developer recognize the aesthetics of landscaping as support for the value of the structure. This gently sloping piece of property had been hand cleared, which opened space for construction while preserving the character of the land. The site was already in the process of refurbishment using ornamentals such as ginger, heliconia, and dwarf banana that would complement the house yet frame the ocean view. Since construction would use more labor than machinery, the plants could become established while the structure took shape.

This sense of order among reform was almost as inspiring as the spectacle I had witnessed the day before, outside the Spanish *escuela* we had begun attending. A colony of leaf cutter ants had been disassembling and moving the leaves and flowers of a massive African tulip tree which shaded the front entrance of the school. Among the constant traffic of giants in this major part of town, a minuscule community had formed a tiny two-lane highway to complete their mission. The sense of order established by the ants, within the chaotic travel of giant feet, was the element essential to completing the monumental task they had chosen.

These observations, each containing similar core values, awakened within me the realization that all of my deadlines were self-imposed, that my perceptions of poor choices were exactly that—perceptions; and that there was no reason why I should not go to Florida to confer with my clients and invite my family to meet me there. I could vacation with them on the beach around my work schedule. That was simple! Is this not what my new life was supposed to be about? Why is it so hard for me to remember? That thought needed to be added to my gratitude list: I am grateful to have chosen to live my life different from the world I knew instead of waiting for some catastrophic accident or health challenge to force me into looking at life differently. I need to take my cue from the people of this coastline and live more in the moment...live in the moment...live....

Julio—July

More to Explore

My Florida excursion went well and gave me much on which to reflect. The trip was intended to renew my visa, see clients and enjoy time with my family. An unexpected aspect was the illumination it brought to the vague undercurrent of dissatisfaction that was at the core of my earlier frustrations. Returning to the manicured environment of the Gulf Coast had given me a feeling of things "unreal" after my six years of separation. It seemed almost a disparity in extreme to the jungles and coastlines of Hawai'i and Honduras, the homes to which I had become accustomed. It was not that one place was better than another; it was more recognizing my realization. I saw the differences as comparable to floating in a pooled area with a trained dolphin, or swimming in the ocean in the company of wild dolphins.

Since April, I had been in the thought process of creating a retreat for the following spring. It would be my first in Honduras. I contacted Oscar to see if he would combine talents, and once that commitment was made, I was under pressure to find properties that could lodge the attendees. My narrow knowledge of the area offered limited choices that I felt would be suitable for my type of retreat experience. As days fell away, I found myself caving in to having to choose a polished tourist accommodation or possibly using my own home; neither idea was rewarding. This "housing" spur was an irritating distraction and fed my feelings of discontent. Ordin had dubbed my retreats "Socio-Eco Tours" because I prefer to allow nature and guidance from traditional elders support the experience that I am sharing with my people. Therefore, the accommodations where the participants stay is as important to the atmosphere as the wisdom shared.

The trip to the U.S. forced me out of my daily environment and brought clarity to my stagnant thinking, just what I needed to recognize my own inner guidance. Then, as though on cue, the day after I arrived back in El Porvenir my neighbors invited Ordin and me to explore some of their favorite areas to see if any of them would enrich the retreat I was planning. It was amazing, and a bit embarrassing, to realize how much I verbalized my thoughts once I realized they had been listening. However, Ordin and I quickly encouraged Pueo through all of her morning routines, set up her food and water stations, and then allowed her to settle in for her eight-hour nap; she would hardly realize we were gone. Then my mate and I were ready to pile into the quad-cab pickup with the family of four that was waiting to show us some of the white sand beaches of tranquil far-off places, before driving to the higher altitudes of Pico Bonito Mountain and a lodge of rustic elegance nestled on the edge of the National Park. It was a wonderland of nature. Beauty and serenity were available at every turn of the head. We walked graveled trails where beautifully colored butterflies and tropical birds flittered through the brush, riding the fragrant breezes of an unspoiled rain forest. One of the winding paths took a turn, which brought the sound of falling water to our ears and finally led us to a pool at the base of a waterfall. This had possibilities!

After exploring the park area, it was time to be off again. Once more the six of us scrambled into the truck; this time we headed for some hot springs outside the town of Sambo Creek. In Hawai'i, I had enjoyed the benefits of these natural, hot springs and similarly formed steam vents; however, I did not realize they could be found in Honduras since the country has no volcanoes. As I questioned our host on the drive out of town, I learned that even though the country has no volcanoes, neighboring countries do. The related movement of the earths crust created the *Nombre de Dios* Mountains and allows for the heat from their lava pools to escape. Subterranean water deposits become heated to almost boiling temperatures before overflowing and beginning their cascade from openings in the mountain, then mixing with the cold water streams produced by the rains at the high peaks. The force of the water creates pools of varying temperatures as it traverses the terrain.

When we arrived at the hot pond area the women and children went to the bathhouse to change into swimsuits while the men picked some ripe *cacao* (chocolate) for snacks before we headed for the pools. This was my first introduction to this tasty treat. I was at first unimpressed at the appearance of the fruit itself as I watched them snap the odd looking green pods from the trees. However, I soon found myself astonished when the barely maturing fruit was split open to expose a white cellulose coating on the seeds that tasted as sweet as strawberries. As we strolled toward a stand of trees, my neighbor explained the pools and property were owned by a woman who had just recently decided to share this family treasure with the rest of the world. She had enhanced the natural amenities by building a cool water pool at the base of the terraced warm ponds and providing horses for trail rides to higher elevations. The children ran ahead of us and the sounds of their laughter and splashing suggested the walk would be only a short distance from where we left our bags and clothes. As we reached the top of a small rise and came in sight of the ponds, the scene took on photo quality. Its pristine condition gave it a timeless appearance. Was this what the first white man saw? Even before the time of the Spanish explorers, this stream had been making its journey from the higher point in the mountain to the lower basin of the coastal area, quietly minding its course in the summer and becoming a raging torrent during the winter storms. The force of this watercourse had forged a trough over the years which now guided the stream from its source through the lush green jungle speckled with wild, red Hibiscus, eventually to spill from under the small wooden bridge before me into the terraced basins formed by stone.

This was not the place to come if one needed sidewalks and handrails. But if one wanted to experience the beauty of nature, gently contoured by someone who loved the land, this was the place. This is what we had entirely to ourselves, except for of the caretaker. We were far from traffic, shopping, and the business of life. What a peaceful sensation: the warm water swirling around me as it cascaded over the stones, its music beginning to lull my mind while my eyes were teased to closing by the dappled sunlight dancing on the water from the arbor canopy above. Add to this picture the aroma and taste of the sweet *cacao* fruit we had eaten and the experience became a reward for each of the five senses.

As with most children, it was less than an hour before they were ready to lead us on an adventure to higher altitudes. We crawled into the pickup again, following the directions of the oldest child, to find the roadbed trail that would lead us to pools farther up the mountain. We let ourselves through the corral of the trail horses, secured the gate, and put the truck into four-wheel drive. We managed to reach the first plateau before it became obvious the heavy spring rains had exposed enough slippery, muddy rock face to make even four-wheel traffic impossible. Now we faced three choices: return to the lower pools (immediately vetoed by the children), rent the trail ride horses, or walk. I could not get excited about the prospect of hiking a terrain that is less than a thirty-degree angle from my face, but somewhere in the back of my mind was a vague childhood memory of riding horseback in a wet swimsuit. The pain I had for weeks from chafed thighs had anchored that experience deeper than any memory of having wind blow in my hair, so I opted for the hike.

It has been thirty years since I quit smoking. But, the congestion from my fifteen-year habit, added to the weak lung tendencies of being born under the sign of Gemini, haunts me each time I attempt any climb. I was determined to make the best of this but, within a short distance, I had already become weary of the extra weight of the towel I had thrown over my shoulder; it was an aggravating addition to my already developing discomfort. Continuing to plod along, I could feel the familiar heat that signaled my face had begun its transition from slightly flushed to an alarming shade of crimson. We were less than halfway into the trek before my heart was racing, my chest hurting and my bronchioles screaming for oxygen. The pain triggered the scolding dialog I reserve for myself in times like these: the "Why did you do this to yourself?" and "Why don't you work out at a gym?" questions. The mental chatter continued as I doggedly placed one foot in front of the other, staggering along a minuscule line between survival and certain doom. All the while, I kept my eyes focused on the ground so I would not be distracted by the gullies and loose stones that were awaiting their opportunity to add to my misery. In front of me, Ordin carried our canvas bag, backpack style, and waited patiently whenever I needed time to calm the racing of my respiratory deficiency. I was sure that he was secretly grateful for my white flag signals. The young mom, on the other hand, her body toned from weeks in the gym, gracefully scaled the path a few meters ahead of us. Her bearing was pleasant and polite as she smiled down on us, waiting at each rest point while I labored to stay among the living. Thankfully, neither of them abandoned me gasping for breath on the side of the trail, even though my rest breaks extended the climb from fifteen to almost twenty-five minutes. Finally, we came to a point where the road forked to the right before it bent to the left and continued up the scale. I was already in prayer the small fork was our destination when the children shot for it. Saved!

As I entered the trail, I could see that it was only a short distance to stairs, cut into the mountain, which would lead us down to a park setting. It looked magnificent and almost made the effort worthwhile. My grip on the staircase handrail was white knuckled as it tried to compensate for my weak knees. Pausing to take advantage of the view saved my ego from further embarrassment as I struggled to regain my composure. Gazing down the stairs, I was surprised to see a natural pool, surrounded on three sides by a manmade boardwalk with a shower and small changing house buried out here in the woods. With my knees and lungs ready to participate in the hike again, I started the descent, aware the children were waiting for their mom to enter the water first. As the mother slid down a large boulder and into the pool, she remarked that the water was much warmer at this altitude than in the pools below. Steam hung in the air behind her where boiling hot water cascaded over stones to meet with the cooler mountain stream. She had found a ledge in the boulder to sit on, which kept her chest and shoulders above the waterline. As the rest of us prepared to enter, she shouted that she had seen something pink in the water at the bottom of the pond. I peered through the rippling water, trying to make out the pink semicircle form that was lying on the bottom. "It must be a snake." she claimed. "That would be strange." I thought, "A pink snake?" The five of us stood around the walkway watching and waiting. No one wanted to enter the water if it was a snake but none of us wanted to be an alarmist. The mom sat on her rock, waiting for some wise sage to confirm or deny her suspicion; should she panic and run or had she misjudged it? Finally, her husband became the man of action and solved the problem by handing her a three-foot stick with which to fish out the object, while the children coached her to contact the strange object. The stick met with success and it began to lift the pink object free from the bottom. As it broke the surface of the water, all of us stared in disbelief. Even without my glasses I could see it certainly was a snake—a small Coral snake. Lifted high above the water, it was still difficult to recognize since, like lobsters and shrimp dunked into boiling water, it had turned pink as it died in the steaming water of the ponds.

Now the children were reluctant to get in the pond and the men were finding other areas of interest. Was I still going to join my friend in the pond? Hmm, one of the things I loved about Hawai'i was the fact of no snakes. One boiled snake led me to believe that any other reptile making the same choice would follow the same fate. I had already faced the issue of snakes when Pu brought one in for examination and the topic of snakes had resolved itself in my mind as being part of where we have chosen to live. Even the Garden of Eden had a snake, so "Move over, *amiga*...I'm coming in".

¿Café?

Our friend, Oscar, has been to visit from Las Vegas. It was so good to see him again. This was his first visit since he helped us settle here six months earlier. We had a lot to catch up on as we realized the number of months that had passed.

During this visit, he introduced us to a Hondureño habit that had escaped our notice all this time, namely "*café hora.*" Around four in the afternoon, many Honduran folks stop what they are doing and take a break with a cup of rich, Honduran coffee and a pastry. Whether they are city folks or live out in the country, this time is set aside to relax, wind down the workday and visit with friends. Many times I have walked to the internet café in town around that time of day and seen folks sitting on chairs or stools under the shade of a mango tree enjoying coffee, conversation and the Caribbean breeze. I had never put two and two together until Oscar pointed it out. I guess the habit would be similar to the English "tea time." Because of the heat of the day, most people will wait until the cooler evening hours for a true supper, so this refresher offers a bit of nourishment to hold them over until the evening meal.

I have adopted the habit and will generally have my coffee Honduran style, which is consumed with sugar and cream. If I drink coffee in the morning, it is invariably unsweetened and black, but this afternoon treat seems to call for a bit of sweetness. The pastries favored by the locals are almost healthy with their minimally processed sugar contents and are the perfect complement to the rich and satisfying coffee. Depending on what my other family members are doing, I may take my break in the hammock on the veranda. This is the place I have chosen to study my Spanish book while I catch the afternoon breeze. I have not returned to Spanish School since coming home from the U.S. last month. I thought I would save myself the frustration of rushing to Ceiba three times a week to become exasperated over my inabilities. I made some English-Spanish flash cards, which Rosanna and I use for memory exercises after lunch and before the cleanup. Once she leaves for home, I continue for another hour with a study guide I found and then spend another half hour or so reviewing during my *café hora*. These two-and-a-half hours a day, with Rosanna's pronunciation guidance, are easier on my nerves and accomplish two goals: they allow me to absorb more of the language at a pace I can deal with and allow Rosanna a chance to study English.

The Mas Excelenté Idea

During the short time that Oscar was with us, one of the projects I asked him to do was to set aside time to help me have a conference with Cesár, then Rosanna. I wanted to make sure that things were going as smoothly as I believed they were, plus discover if there was something more that these two needed...something the language barrier restricted asking.

We held the first conference under the shade of the gazebo in the late afternoon, the day after Oscar arrived. Ordin, Oscar, Cesár, and I sipped *cervezas* and laughed as we recounted the uncertainty and confusion that had filled so many of our days over the last six months. After we had laughed ourselves to silence telling stories on each other, I asked Oscar to inquire of Cesár if there was anything he needed to tell us while we had an able translator. I wish I could have recorded Cesár's response to the question. His words were beautiful and heartfelt, more touching than any greeting card. Don Cesár wanted me to know that I had been a great influence on him and the yard and that I had awakened the fruit trees, which were now in blossom and fruiting for the first time. Also, through my example, he had learned to meet each morning with a smile and a sunny attitude, no matter what was going on in his life. He finished by saying that it was a pleasure to come to work when the property owners are interested in the grounds and willing to supply the necessities he required to maintain it. My English paraphrase can never do his words the justice they deserve. I was so touched by the sincerity of his words that my limited response of *muy amable* caught in my throat; he was being more than kind.

The meeting with Rosanna went a bit differently. Oscar had to cut short his time with us to complete some dental work he had started over on the Pacific side of the country. Running short of opportunities, I asked Oscar to present the same question to Rosanna while the four of us were ending lunch the day before he was to leave. Her response was to start weeping and telling us the sadness that existed in her extended family. She said that she needed to do more to help them, and was asking for more money or she would need to find another job. She was willing to work more hours, but she needed more money. This was not at all what I expected to hear! She had just received the promised three-month raise with her June salary. Not only did she just get the raise before my trip, but I was very disappointed to learn that she had taken off work during most of the week I was in Florida. That was only two weeks after her raise took effect. The week after I returned, she got an infection in her foot from standing for hours on end while cooking and serving at her sister's wedding reception; that required another week off from work. Now she wanted another raise? Oscar attempted to comfort Rosanna while trying to offer me counsel on Honduran domestics, but within this chaos, a quiet within me allowed me to understand what I must do.

I asked Oscar to explain to Rosanna how much we enjoyed having her as part of our household, as well as what a wonderful cook she was. I had him explain that she was worth much more money than we could ever pay her, but we were limited by what we could financially afford. It was important for her to know there would be raises in the future but this was not the time. If she had truly found a job that was going to pay her the substantial increase she was asking, I would understand her wanting to leave, and I was more than willing to write a letter of recommendation for her. She would go with our blessings. I asked Oscar to let her know that we would honor whatever decision she made. She wiped her eyes and thanked us for our kindness and understanding; she would consider her options and let us know her decision...and then we waited.

In the month since that conference, nothing more was said. Ordin made a point to pick up some rice, flour, sugar, salt, and cornmeal when he stopped by the grocery one afternoon before coming home. He presented them to Rosanna with instructions to take them to her family when she went to visit them again. We asked don Cesár to be thinking of someone to fill Rosanna's position should she choose to leave, and then left it to resolve itself. I knew this was a big decision for her, torn between wanting to help improve the circumstances of her relatives and not wanting to give up a position where she was so well treated. The work contract we had agreed on was created around our mutual needs. It allowed her time in the morning to get her little family ready for the day, as well as getting home early enough to be wife and mother before attending night school. Her wages were above average for a domestic and did not require a full day of labor. Our contract also gave her weekends off and time away when there was illness at home. These are the benefits that would be sacrificed for the extra six hundred fifty Lempiras—roughly thirty-five dollars—which she was planning to give to extended family. These were heavy issues to weigh.

There is a saying that the seeds of greatness exist in all of us, and that given fertile soil they will sprout. Possibly the desire for more money and the willingness to do more work were the fertile ground for Rosanna's *mas excelenté* idea. *Fútbol* is very popular here and, during one of her visits with her mother, she suddenly became aware of the great number of people who sit around watching the game. She decided to try packaging some of her homemade food items to sell as a concession. It took foresight and courage to step out as a businesswoman in our little rural area since this is a country that offers scant opportunities for women. Now she and her little daughter are vending pastries and snacks at the ballgames one Sunday each month. What a wonderful opportunity for Rosanna and what an excellent example for her daughter. With a little bit of coaching, she is learning to carefully portion out the proceeds to restock her supplies, have some money to spend and a portion to save. The response to this idea has given her the courage to see past her present circumstances, as well as permission to dream. Her first dream is to have a new stove in her own name. I think she has a brilliant idea, and if she can hold tight to her dream, I believe she will be a success.

Check and Double Check

Police checkpoints are common in this country. There is one between the airport in La Ceiba and the turn to El Porvenir. It is quite intimidating to see these officers, with guns strapped to their hips and machine guns in hand, waving traffic aside for inspection. Some of the officers are local traffic police, some agricultural inspectors, and some national police. The nationals are usually the ones with machine guns. Ordin has done most of the driving since we moved here, in part because he likes to and because the less-than-orderly flow of traffic keeps me in apprehension just riding as a front-seat passenger. We cannot get to Ceiba or the airport without passing the checkpoint, so we have had many opportunities to see these men in action.

The number of times we have been stopped for examination is very limited and since we always have our automobile papers, passports, and U.S. driver's licenses, they generally send us through. I remember the first time we were flagged to stop; my mind was racing as to what infraction of the law we could have committed while I reached into my purse to retrieve my papers. I did my best to appear calm while practicing my *"Buenos dias!"* but my light, gringo face must have taken on a ghostly shade of pale as we babbled *"El Porvenir."* and *"No comprende."* to the questions that he asked. Since we were OBVIOUSLY tourists, he sent us through.

I have seen folks waved to the side and required to completely empty their trunk of belongings so they could be searched; I believe that would have to be a very frightening experience. Of course, there have also been days when everyone had to stop because the local police officers were selling traffic safety books, similar to the U.S. Rules of the Road paperback, so for a small donation of one hundred Lempiras you could continue your journey. After four months, we had collected three of these Spanish language instruction books so I suggested to Ordin that we show them to the officer instead of buying another when they are offered. Following my suggestion, but not to the letter, on the next occasion that Ordin was stopped and offered booklets he did his best to explain to the officer. Using his best Spanish and hand gestures, Ordin explained that he already had a couple; the result of that communication was that Ordin ended up paying for two of the little books. Now he travels with them in the car, and if he gets stopped, he waves them at the officer selling the books. They both smile and laugh as he is allowed to pass.

The last time Ordin flew to Florida to renew his visa, we had to travel to the airport before five in the morning. This would be my first time to drive a Honduras highway. I was a little apprehensive but I told myself there would be next to no traffic at that time of the day and the little trip would be smooth sailing. Ordin drove to the airport and I noticed with some surprise the checkpoint was well lit, but we were of little interest to the uniformed officers drinking coffee and we cruised past, hesitating only for the speed bumps. The security gate at the airport was still tied open at this early hour so it took no time at all to arrive at the departure gate and say good-bye to my loved one. As I walked around the little Sport and entered the driver's side, the voice in my head chastised me for not familiarizing myself with the control panel of the car the day before. With Ordin doing all the driving, I never had a need to do so; now, in the darkness of the predawn, that suggestion would have been a good one to follow.

Even slipping on my glasses did not help me identify which gears were where, so I allowed the car to drift forward until I was under the yellow glare of a parking lot light and able to read the letters on the shifter. Once I was sure that I was not going to burn out first gear, my confidence returned and I proceeded to follow the exit signs to the highway and continued the short journey to Porvenir. It felt good to be behind the wheel again. No sooner had I made the left turn onto the highway than an early morning rain shower began. "Oh damn, where are the windshield wipers?" I mumbled in the darkness. Fumbling with controls, I found the high beams and washed the windshield before looking up to see that I was entering the police checkpoint and being waved to the side. "Oh, no, now what do I do?" I thought as I maneuvered the car off the road and searched for the window controls. They do not work on the passenger side of the car so I was totally inexperienced in knowing whether they lifted back or tilted forward. I could hear the officer blowing his whistle and I was pretty sure I saw him gesturing through the rain spotted windows. My anxiety to open the window and grope for my papers while recalling my stumbling Spanish was compounded by the poor visibility in the rainy darkness and kept me unsure of what he was signaling I should do. Finally, the window responded to my frantic button fumbling, and as it smoothly slid down its grooves, the officer waving and walking toward the car came into enough clarity for me to recognize that he was only signaling me to go on. He had remembered the auto as part of the local traffic. What a relief! When I arrived home and closed the huge, metal gate behind me, I felt like a rabbit that had safely made it back to burrow. As good as it was to survive being challenged to a new level of growth; I knew I needed to get out more.

agosto — August

The Turning Point

That highway experience and a later call for help from our Hawai'i 'ohana brought about the illumination I had been asking for. Just a few days after Ordin's return, an e-mail came from a friend in Hilo describing symptoms that her nine-year-old daughter was experiencing. Among others, the young girl was refusing to eat for fear of choking. The mother thought the girl had scratched her throat and was allowing her to eat only soft foods such as applesauce and pudding to offer time for healing, but she found the situation was not improving. As I read her e-mail and discussed it with Ordin, we came to the realization that these were symptoms of anorexia. After I responded to her e-mail, explaining our beliefs and other symptoms to watch for, it was only hours before the mother emailed to confirm our suspicions.

The mother explained that, while waiting for my first response, she had taken her daughter to a doctor who had found no sign of strep or disease yet had prescribed an antibiotic as a "shotgun" approach to the symptoms. The lack of disease and the confirmation of the list of behavior oddities we had warned of proved to the mother that we were on the right track. I sent a list of suggested foods for the child, foods that would keep her protein level high enough to prevent muscle mass from wasting. I then turned my attention to what I felt was the cause of this heartbreaking situation and what I felt was the only possible solution.

Anorexia is a disease of the twenty-first century. It is only since our society started marketing ultra thin bodies and the fear of obesity in the seventies that this choking disease has developed. Before that time, our sex symbols wore size 14 and 16 clothing, and earlier in history our models of feminine beauty were more "Rubenesque", so named for the nudes painted by the famous artist Rubens and others of his time. As the young women of the seventies became influenced by the fashions of their time, a fear-terror of not being acceptable developed, and subsequently an entire industry developed to support it. There is an adage that we will always realize our greatest fear, meaning that we help create what we are most afraid of, in part because we program it into the unconscious thoughts that whisper to us twenty-four/seven. It becomes part of our conversation, our behavior and then our choices. As these young women of the seventies became mothers, their influence on their young children imprinted the obsession as well as the terror, and terror constricts the throat.

The form of this beautiful Hawaiian mother of four had progressively softened with each baby, compounded by her islander's love of local foods. The sturdy genes of the Polynesians are an oxymoron to the magazine model image, and the islander's love of life (and food) should be what sets them free from the influence of western society, but logic cannot always override emotions.

With food suggestions for the daughter, I sent directions for the mother that would help her redirect her own obsession with trying to regain her pre-marriage form. Sometimes profound realization is enough to release the emotional hold, but most often the fear is so deeply programmed into our behavior that it requires redirecting. Fear is a powerful force and this is why it is so often employed to control behavior. Simply to try to stop fear/terror is as futile as trying to hold back the flow of lava. My suggestion to the mother was to begin exploring information on fungus and a condition called candida, which would probably be the cause of her weak body tone. As she begins to recognize the connection, it would become her new "crusade"...a more positive term than obsession. This new interest would become the focus of her conversation and attention instead of the negative one about her weight. The fresh information would also lead her, and subsequently her family, into a healthier lifestyle. Planting the seeds of "balance" into the fertile mind of her daughter would offer a healing path that would be constructive instead of destructive.

I explained to the mother that this concept was called "star medicine." The direction of most modern medicine is primarily to focus on treating the symptoms of a condition, while the holistic approach explores the cause of dis-ease. Unfortunately both systems spotlight, or feed, attention to the negative situation. Star medicine, on the other hand, places attention on the desired outcome. Recent scientific research supports the concept that the mind creates an image based on its perception of information offered. This is why two different people can have two different reactions to the same situation. Since thoughts are energy, we project them into the universe like an antenna, with the resulting outcome being "like energy attracts." This is the foundation of positive imaging as taught by teachers of affirmative thinking all around the globe. This system ignites the natural healer within us, which is needed to make any of the other modalities truly effective. This concept has been hidden in the teachings of Hawaiian kahuna as well as Australian aboriginals.

Working with the mother and child brought me to a realization about my reactions to the challenges in my new life. Not wanting to become aware of my state of fear, I had created a supporting case for my beliefs, similar to a lawyer swaying a jury. I had distorted the evidence to support my viewpoint. That realization had the impact of a tsunami, ripping through the protective barrier I had placed around the classified files of my recollections from the last few months. The impact laid bare the judgments and perceptions that I had unconsciously created to sustain my negative concepts. Witnessing each of these circumstances while they spilled through my awareness helped me realize how these altered perceptions had fed a belief that was undermining my self-image. Whatever the cause, my release would come, just like this family, by placing my focus on who I want to be. In doing this, I would begin to see situations differently, and therefore react in a way to support the new belief which would change the outcome. I would need new images to override the old negative ones.

I began by discussing with Ordin the designs for a house we had talked about building on the beach. I love the design of the house we have but incorporating a little Hawai'i and some old Florida "cracker" charm could make it better. I started to see us living in the house and Pueo playing in the yard. I created in my mind the image of myself in cool summer linen, driving through La Ceiba, and talking to tradespersons in fluent Spanish. I saw myself at local soccer games and social events, truly immersed in the local culture. I decided to start walking in the evenings again, a habit I had lost sometime after moving here; that would put me in touch with more neighborhood people. To support all these new images, I placed pictures around the bedroom and bath to reflect my new focus. I also picked up some drafting paper so Ordin and I could start designing our dream home at a more tangible level. After weeks of chanting, asking and praying, the Divine had guided friends in need to bring the answer I had been searching for. I had a new direction and a star to follow.

A New Pu Too

My heart has gone out to Pueo a number of times. Watching her deal with and process all these new experiences has been an emotionally wrenching situation for us. The move from her jungle haunts to the confining, walled security of this new place must depress her with its limits. Many people do not believe animals have feelings but I know they do. The days that Pu sleeps the entire time are the days she is feeling sad. She will not initiate play, sit on my desk and talk, or supervise Ordin's projects; she just sleeps. I have found that we can help her through these times with something new to investigate. In our old home she was always exploring the undergrowth, watching doves take dust baths in the red cinder road, or catching tiny mice in the rocks and undergrowth. The manicured setting of this new home offers few places to become safely camouflaged for observation. Don Cesar and I have begun slowly expanding the gardens from single plantings against the wall, to orderly lush scenery of varied heights and density.

Pueo was happy to be in the garden with me again in the cool morning hours. This is something she and I were in the habit of doing in our old life. She was intrigued with the new gardens and plantings until she found herself challenged for space. This Atlántida coast has a species of crab that burrows inland from the river. It, like most of the animal life here, fears no one. None of the animals appear aggressive; each species goes about meeting its own needs, but even the tiny birds stand their ground if they feel challenged. These birds scold Pu for lying under the hibiscus tree when they want to feed. One day a hummingbird, frustrated from its efforts to move Pu, flew within inches of our noses to chastise us for her insolence. It is a weird sensation when a hummingbird gets into your face. The need for survival is so basic here there is no place for timidity. Our Hawai'i cat is a timid soul. The size of these birds belies their intimidation, but the crabs are a different story. The crabs stay underground most of the day, but during the night and early morning, they come out to explore the vegetation. The locals hunt them as a source of food by holding a stick down into the burrow. The crab grabs the stick with its vise-like claw and will not release while there is tension. Pueo also loves to be out in the cool of evening and early morning, and of course, becomes intrigued by anything that rustles the bushes.

It is her nature to offer to play with most life-forms that share her surroundings, so I am sure this is how the crab latched onto the ruff of her neck. Her yowl snapped Ordin and me out of bed and onto the veranda, passing a dark streak as she flew through the cat door, with nothing left to explain the commotion except a tuft of fur. It was not until the next morning, when Ordin found the crab still trying to escape the second floor veranda, that the entire story became clear.

Oscar had told me that most Hondureños do not like cats, and I have found that it is because they are afraid of them. The poverty level makes it prohibitive for many folks to afford to care for pets, yet because there is little spaying and neutering, the animals exist. A community of people and their rubbish is the easiest guarantee of food, so these animals share whatever humans can give them in exchange for a rodent-free environment, security, and protection. The few cats that I have seen around town have the same independence as the crabs; when villagers have tried to touch them or pick up kittens, they are invariably bitten. This is the training Rosanna had with cats before coming to Pueo's home.

Pueo is finicky about strangers and Rosanna was cautious of cats; this was not a winning combination but I felt that over time, each would accept the other. When I returned from taking my group on retreat to Mexico, Pueo's behavior told me that I had only thought I was in touch with my feelings. When Rosanna came in the gate each morning, Pu went into the closet...and there she would stay unless I was going to be in the room. Along with this behavior, Pu would no longer nap on the sofa in our bedroom, as had been her habit, and she gave a wide berth whenever the broom was brought into use. All of this was starting to paint a pretty clear picture of the perils of Pueo. I needed to address this, and soon, but how would be my challenge. I looked up the Spanish word for daughter (*hija*) and asked Rosanna if her *hija* was *numero uno en tu casa*? She smiled with pride and agreed that yes, her four-year-old daughter was the most important person in their home. I then told her Pueo, *la gata*, was *numero uno* at this *casa*. Next, I picked up the dish towel and, while shaking my head and saying "*¡No!.*", swished the towel as though to chase something away. I then took the broom from her hand and acted out chasing something with it while shaking my head and repeating *"¡No!."* She looked surprised that I knew what she had done, so I told her *"Pueo habla me."* Pueo told me. She nodded her head to let me know that she understood, implying that it would not happen again. Here, almost five months later, Rosanna has overcome her fear of Pu but our feline still views Rosanna as one of the hazards of Honduras.

In all, I believe Pu has done well. She did not get to vote on the idea of moving, but as pampered as we treat her, she would have been devastated if left behind. She has become accustomed to the noises of her Honduran neighborhood and has accepted don Cesar's quiet manner. She has learned about snakes and crabs, and had her first wasp sting. Thunder is still a frightening issue, but otherwise, she is spending more and more time outdoors; by next summer she should acclimate to the heat. So, as traumatic as each of these incidents was in its moment, our little girl has shown the heart of a lion by staying the mark. The three of us comfort each other through the hard times and play together in the good times; we belong together...we are family.

More on Animals

My first negative impression, the day I arrived in Honduras, was the condition of the animals that I saw roaming the roads and byways. The sight of so many seemingly neglected animals would dismay most Americans. We are accustomed to seeing more fat and sheen on our four-legged amigos; to our way of thinking, dirt and bones represent neglect.

The condition of the animals is reflective of the economic situation. The more affluent class of people has the money to lavish the best of care on their horses, dogs and cattle; the less fortunate can only share the little they have. In both cases, the animal is getting the best that their person has to offer. I have never seen an animal here tethered where it could not get to food or water, or where it had to lay in its own excrement. I do not believe that even the poorest person would deliberately let an animal starve; however, means are meager through much of the country and humans take care of their families first.

The young mom and her family brought home two *toro niños*—baby bulls—a couple of months ago. They were both milk babies and one was still in the wobble-legged stage. The dairy farmer who owned the herd they were born into could not afford the loss of milk to calves that would not become milk producers themselves. The choice was butcher them at one month, as milk-fed veal, or separate them from their mothers and offer them a chance to survive. He set pans of milk on the ground twice a day but it was up to the bulls to learn to drink from the pan and start to eat grass. In the U.S. they might have been killed at birth, so which is more humane? With this farmer, he was more than happy to give them to someone who wanted them. I guess the real prize is not in being given life but in being given the opportunity to live.

Horses are often a necessity of life along this coast; they are more durable than a bicycle and offer more choices. Some owners stake their horses along the highway to feed. This expands the grazing area of the horse and benefits the community by clearing the roadside of high grass for pedestrian traffic. The highway dust and accompanying parasites exact a toll on these roadway veterans, as well as the occasional fatality when a horse snaps a tether. The sight of horses as a daily function of life was a unique experience for me when I first arrived. Now there is a certain sense of balance in watching them pull carts or carry riders among the automobile traffic while transporting firewood or produce around town. I especially enjoy seeing the foals that escort their moms to work. Their alert, young eyes seem filled with wonder as they stand close to their mothers' protective sides. In Porvenir there are always horses roaming loose. Like many the dogs and an occasional calf, I never know if they have owners at all. These horses perform the same task along our dusty roadways, keeping vegetation down while the dogs snag any rodents or lizards the grazing *caballos* may have disturbed. The shaggy appearance of the nomads had me wanting to give each a handful of grain with a bath and curry when I first arrived. Since then I have learned an appreciation and respect for the balance that exists here.

It was after I saw a horse with a grossly deformed front leg, grazing along a row of shops on an entry street to Ceiba, when I began to pay enough attention to offer reform to my perspective. The first time I saw the Palomino it was tied outside a store, grazing on a patch of grass. Its left foreleg bent in a forty-five-degree angle above the fetlock; the bend formed the current walking surface. I was appalled. The second time I saw him, he was in a shady pasture around the corner and down the street from the first. This time there was no lead; he was grazing freely. With more opportunity to study the horse, I realized the horse's leg must have been broken when it was very young for it to have callused to that degree. In some other place the colt would probably have been shot. The horse's owners may have tried to splint the break but did not have the money or training to give it the care necessary to insure healing; nonetheless, the horse was allowed to live. If the owners did not have the money to properly splint the horse, they probably did not geld him; with his coloring he could be prized for breeding. He does not appear to be in pain. Was it the right decision? Just like the baby bulls, this horse was given the opportunity to live.

Life is a struggle for many of the people in this country and that struggle is the common bond between man and beast. They understand each other and work together to that end. Dogs in the street never harass me as they did while walking my neighborhood roads in Hawai'i, yet I hear them protecting their homes from stray cattle and people who approach their owners' doors without notice. Every soul is working; the geese and chickens that forage for bugs along the road in front of the house live in symbiosis with the folks who offer them sanctuary. I cannot say that animals are never exploited or abused as they have been in more evolved areas, but I am learning a new appreciation based on the spirit of an animal as opposed to only its appearance. As many of our modern prophets teach, life is all about the journey, not the destination.

Red Rubber Boots in the Caribbean

It is mid-August and the topic of conversation around Porvenir is *lluvia*: rain. There has been a lot of precipitation in the mountains and surrounding areas but it has been unseasonably dry for the last three weeks. This is the time of year when evening rains are anticipated to restore vitality to the vegetation after the heat of the day. Living in a rural community, the subject of rain can always be relied on as a topic of common interest. However, with the change of seasons, this matter has taken on a new point of interest; something more of a prophetic warning. It seems October through January is normally cold and rainy. Now, when it comes to talking about cold with Caribbean Coast Hondurans, I am afraid that I will have to test their opinions with time. During this season, I have been sweltering in the heat and watched them go about their daily activities in jeans and sometimes long-sleeve wear, concerned only about covering their heads. Thus, when they hold their arms in mock shivers to describe the coastal winter, I foresee finding my comfort zone. Where I give their experience credit is on the subject of flooding.

With the ocean as a near neighbor and a river outside my back door, I do not think I can discount the experience of the locals. Flooding was one of the concerns that we had questioned Kent about when we were considering the purchase of the house. The country was already experiencing winter storms when he inspected the property for us, and U.S. news coverage was reporting that many bridges washed out in Honduras. Kent explained the swollen tributaries were caused by the volume of rain in the mountains as well as the lowlands. With so much water coming so quickly, it was impossible for the waterways to contain it. He explained that with our river, it was fed by an underground source so it would seldom rise above its banks. With the small amount that I could understand of don César's narrative, this information was confirmed. However, in some of César's story, there was the warning that storms coming in from the ocean, as with a hurricane, could choke the river. With the river's natural course blocked, it would start to rise over its banks and begin filling the back of our yard. Then there was also the other river that ran along the pineapple fields outside town to the west; it was mountain fed and invariably flooded enough of the town to run under our front gate and fill the front yard. Each of these stories, plus the one about canoeing through town after Hurricane Mitch blew through, was making me thankful for my two-story home and spurring my brain into emergency awareness mode. A mental checklist, which explored ways to block up the car and raise the downstairs beds, was already underway.

I could also see where a small butane stove, and some warm, flannel lounge clothes might be nice to have. If water was going to keep me in, I wanted to be comfortable. From that point, my mind suggested boots. This thought ran fingernails across the blackboard of my childhood memories. My first memory of boots was the black rubber boots with buckles up the front. They were effective in the snow but hardly a fashion statement. Next, my memory flashed a picture of the red rubber boots I was presented with while I was in third grade. My insecure self-esteem found them barely acceptable since most of the girls in my class had given up wearing red boots by second grade. Nevertheless, they were such an improvement over the black, buckle type that I do not remember complaining a lot about them, other than when they would rub and chafe the back of my calves. I was glad when we moved to an area where we were required to ride a bus and no longer had to deal with the boots for school issue. By high school, we had moved again and we were back in snow country. I also had a one-mile walk to school, so I needed boots.

I can only remember one time, before my sophomore year of high school, when I was a participant in shopping for school clothes. With six kids, Mom found it easier to shop for us during her lunch breaks at work; she could always return the following day anything that did not fit. So imagine my dismay when I opened my bag of school apparel and found it included red rubber boots! I was horrified. I would look like an emergency signal...a beacon of scarlet color (face included)... as I WALKED the long, lonely mile to my NEW SCHOOL in my FRESHMAN YEAR wearing **BRIGHT RED RUBBER BOOTS!** I did everything I could, short of walking barefoot on the ice, to not have to wear those boots...but to no avail. Every other freshman girl who did not step out of her family car wearing hose and flats was shod in short, black leather boots with soft fur tops and lining.

Thankfully, my last two years of high school were in an area that had plenty of winter cold but very little snow so I was spared any discussion on "goulashes", plus I was working, driving, and buying my own school clothes. By the seventies, I was a mother and needed to set the example for my three children but I did it with fashion boots. Florida set me free of boots and I thought Hawai'i would have also, but once we bought our acre of jungle paradise, Ordin felt my feet needed protection as I stomped through the tangled brush swinging a machete. I knew he was right but I dreaded my choices. There would be no designer boots here, and anytime I got near the display at the garden store the hair on the back of my neck would stand on end. I was managing to make-do in an old pair of tennis shoes until one day my beloved came home with matching, his and her, black, knee-high, rubber boots—the kind that pig farmers wear.

Now it is up to me. Luckily, my visa is due to expire before the rainy season gets under way and I will head for the U.S. to visit friends or family. Each time I make one of these trips, I take a shopping list of things we need that are not available here. I have already started writing the list that will go with me this time. Near the top of this list is boots—rubber boots. It makes perfect sense to me, that with the upcoming weather conditions, there can be no other rational choice, and since I am the one shopping, I just may look around to see if they still make red ones.

SECTION IV

The Outcome

Safety and Security

The choice to move to this part of the world was a step in faith. Many a naysayer had offered rationale against the idea, even suggesting that the country was not safe, but Ordin and I felt that there were unspoken opportunities available here and it seemed important that we should open that particular door for growth.

Now, months after our arrival here, the memory of their words was being tickled out of the dense file of mental material stored in my gray cells. Why these thoughts now? At some level, all mankind seeks security or safety, right? This was where my sequence of thought was guiding me one afternoon as I sat watching our teacher conjugate verbs on the dry wipe board that we had hung under the steps of our patio. Ordin and I had recently renewed our dedication to become competent in the language with the discovery of this lean, young, Hondureño father from Porvenir. He was willing to come to our house two to three times a week to meet with us under the canopy on our patio. His wit, charm, and artistic skill had added a new interest to the drudgery of memory work; yet, my overloaded mind was still seeking a direction for creative avoidance when its quest revealed the subject of safety. Given the choice, my mind elected to follow the path of old memories as a break from the burden of accepting new, and I surrendered to that line of thought.

Without the assurance of safety our minds never feel free to follow higher tendencies, many of which assure security. The higher thoughts related to the subtle energies involved in Feng Shui, ceremonies and blessings are all included in this. Experience indicates that it is only in the pursuit of greater ideals that life takes on its true meaning. So, seeking pleasure through decisions based on safety is a process fraught with conflict. As each of these profound segments of information stepped forward in my mind, offering themselves for consideration, a gallery of faces from my past glided ghost-like against the background; silent witnesses to the truthful direction of my thoughts. Each face offered tribute to a life that had lived under the shroud of protection, believing it to be the path to happiness. It was surprising to realize how many of these lives had left this plane of existence in the instant of one breath, like the blowing out of a candle. If they had it to do again, would they choose to live their lives differently?

Moving to a country whose inhabitants speak a language unlike my own became a pry bar that forced me from my level of safety and security. My confidence came from my experiences and travels that had either been within the shelter of an English-speaking group, or through a country accustomed to my language. With the safety net of language no longer available, this Gemini was left with a sensation as comfortable as walking a high-wire over a canyon during an earthquake. I could see why the island of Roatan had become so popular with many Americans who chose to make Honduras their home; its inhabitants are English speaking.

This reminded me of a favorite local Hawai'i story about a woman who had moved to the remote South Point area of The Big Island in pursuit of UFOs. She was an enthusiast and moved there because of the number of supposed sightings. After months of construction her home was finished and she moved in, thrilled at expecting the extraterrestrial traffic. On her initial evening in her new home, she walked out onto the large lanai to sit with the full panoramic view of the ocean and await the first sighting. The story is that she got her wish; out of the ocean arose a large UFO. The woman got up from her chair, walked through the house to her car and drove away, never to return. It is quite one thing to think you want something, and quite another to come face to face with it.

I guess this was similar to many of my feelings connected with being in Honduras and working through communication difficulties. There were days when I would walk out on the veranda, breathe in the air and thank my Creator for the privilege of being part of this beauty, and there were other moments when I would find myself wondering how much longer do we have to do this. Over the weeks that I began to recognize these fears, I had stumbled onto the realization that fear of speaking another language was one of them. Why did I think there would be something wrong with me if I do not speak English?

Hidden and misunderstood as our fears sometimes are, it is always in the realization of them that our freedom comes, and with the light of that understanding I broke free of my resistance to learning Spanish. I had only thought I wanted to learn Spanish all these years, because if it had truly been my desire, I would have found a way to do it. The frustration from denying my delusion, of feeling that I was not intelligent enough to "get it", was so much more painful than the fear that the truth was finally shoved to the surface.

Like a dark cloud passing from over the house, the release of this belief had a profound effect on my entire household. Rosanna became delighted because I was holding conversations with her; don César began to compliment me on my language skills after many of our morning chats. I found myself free from the reluctance to travel without an English-speaking amigo, but the greatest gift was in the shift of perspective. I began seeing daily experiences differently. The shift gave me a unique insight into the lives of my neighbors. I can only relate this understanding to finding oneself performing an action that you had seen a parent or teacher in the habit of doing, and in repeating that action there is often a flash of insight—an intense understanding about that person, almost as though for one instant in time you and the other person are one. It becomes a window to see the world through the eyes of another, which always offers understanding.

How each person chooses to live out their life is a personal decision and a Divine gift. For me, part of living is striving to learn. I feel that I do that best by putting myself in situations that demand I search the deep well within myself to find the inner strength that allows me to break through that moment. The gift of insight into who I am becoming is always the reward for my struggles. It confirms my belief that if I have only one week, or one day, or one hour left to my life, I need to continue to follow my heart instead of somebody else's rules.

The Final Chapter

In the early predawn, as Pueo and I unlock the gates, turn off the security lights and explore the grounds, there is a comforting reassurance in the noises that have become the familiar sounds of a new day beginning. In the distance, I hear the sound of the surf hitting the beach; the *vaca* across the way are beginning their low mooing as they await the sound of the dairyman opening the gate. Every variety of bird is awakening in its order, heralding the day in joint effort with the chorus of roosters that proclaim the approach of sunrise each morning. Their vocal relay runs from one corner of town to the other for hours before earliest light. The first of the local buses will soon begin its route, sounding its horn for a hundred yards or so before each stop while its full gross weight compresses the river stone of the roadbed; in all, creating a sound that evokes a memory of the rail traffic outside my grandmother's house many years ago. The combination of grinding crunch and blare gave my first morning in Porvenir the confirmation needed to support the belief that trains traveled through the town. Our Ladies of Lactose will pass our *porton* soon. The delicate ballet of their ankles as they move gracefully past the solid middle of our metal gate is a visible testament to the time of day. This daily passing has fixed itself as a familiar timepiece in Pueo's morning, but the days are numbered for this ritual. American developers have bought the land across the river where generations of cows have spent their days grazing. Now the builders want to build condominiums and the dairymen were given six months to find other pastures. Time is running out for Our Ladies.

The neighbors in the enclave are awakening. I hear them splashing water in their morning basin ritual and chopping wood for the cook fire. Where else could I live in the comfort of a summer beach house flanked on one side by folks who sleep in hammocks, use wood for cooking, and have no need for hot water; while the affluence that allows for servants, horses, air conditioning, and all of the other luxuries of the western world are contained on the other. These circumstances may not be as unique as the fact that it all works so well here. Each lifestyle accepts the other.

There is an interesting term we often heard used among locals in Hawai'i; it is "no need", which implies that no effort is required. Within a family or connected circle of friends, when one person owns an object similar to what another needs, there is "no need" to go out and buy one since what one person possesses is equally shared by all. In our Porvenir community, it is not so much a "no need" situation but a matter of economics. The majority of people here cannot afford to have on hand what some future necessity might cause them to need. When a neighborhood child has a flat tire on a bicycle and does not own a pump, the child pushes the bike to the home of someone who would most likely have a source of compressed air. There is no other relationship required other than the one of need and the willingness to help.

In the first few months that we lived in the community, we only knew of one family who personally owned an electrical generator. As frequently as the community loses electricity, the expense involved in buying auxiliary equipment does not really justify the cost for most families. When power goes out, everyone in town shifts to a slower pace and life continues; however, during one power outage, there was a life struggling to continue. One of the women in town had been diagnosed with a terminal condition and on oxygen at home. The oxygen was delivered through a trachea tube in her throat, which was also the vehicle to remove accumulated fluid from her lungs. It was necessary to remove the fluid every three hours to keep her from drowning. All of her breathing and clearing was sustained by an electrically operated machine. One Sunday morning the electricity went off before seven and within minutes the condition of the woman became critical and the family was called together. Her frail condition made it impossible to try to move her while the tropical temperature was a heavy weight upon her chest. Word circulated through the community and someone, somewhere, remembered the family with the generator. The woman's husband went to make the request and the generator was transported back to his home.

Living in this community has offered me the opportunity to see my values through the eyes of people who have much fewer material things than I do but whose lives seem so full. The value of family and community was an important lesson taught by the Hawaiians and Mayans, but my time in Honduras has helped me to recognize that appreciating family and community is intimately entwined with the principle of acceptance. The interdependency of many Honduran communities requires recognizing the essence of a person, which necessitates seeing beyond anomalous behavior. While acceptance does not entail condoning conduct that might be hurtful, it does require understanding that we all have quirks. The people of the community have helped me make this transition from who I was into what is essential here. Their subtle teaching by example became the webbing that bonded me to the community. This, with the support of the young mother, don Cesár, and Rosanna, has helped dissolve many cultural differences. This community of folks, whose support bolstered our struggling efforts to learn Spanish and step into the neighborhood, was similar to parents supporting a toddler's effort in its desire to learn to walk.

Before we moved here, I would never have considered myself a fearful person. Many people think that just making the move was a sign of courage, but I now realize that what I felt as courage was only a surface covering—like armor. As long as I stayed within the safety of what I knew, it would never need to be tested. The move to Honduras stripped away the protective veneer, exposing the metal of who I am. In doing that, I was challenged to examine what I had learned and what I held dear and determine what I truly believed. I once heard that the person who descended the mountain is never the same person who has climbed it, and these words often flashed through my mind when I questioned our decision to move here.

Now we are moving into the seasons of gratitude and brotherly love. As the temperature is cooling and the days grow shorter, I find myself thinking of how we have spent the holidays in the States and wondering what the people of the coastline here do. I think that I want to hold an open house—a *fiesta* of gratitude for all of our neighbors and new friends. For years it has been our habit to decorate the house modestly with flowers and lights for the holidays, but on this occasion I want lots of lights, decorations, music, and food throughout the entire downstairs carport-patio. The wall should be transformed and the gates thrown open. For this one evening I want no physical barriers between my *casa* and all of our friends and neighbors. I would like this occasion to express my appreciation for all that they have done.

So, if you find yourself in Honduras, visiting the area of El Porvenir a couple of days before Christmas, come by and join our festivities.

There are no addresses here; just ask for the *gringos de Hawai'i*. We are on the road to the beach, just down from "Tilapias" restaurant. The gates will be open and the music and laughter will guide you to us. My desire is that this *fiesta* will become a beautiful tradition, since you see, this may be the final chapter in this book, but it is not the end of the story.

Honduras is now my home.

END

Contact

http://www.Gringos-in-Paradise.com

Malana Ashlie at: pathways2@hotmail

Phone: 011-504-429-2369

Ordin Ashlie at: omporvenir@hotmail.com

Phone: 011-504-9961-9404